"Phil Parker has a way with words
command of your emotions, feeling

Prof Dan Moerman, Autho

"The dû is an essential tool in any ุ......
the perspective I needed to continue."

Ed Stafford, the first man to walk the entire length of the
Amazon

"Phil Parker's latest book is extremely educational and presents a
practical philosophy on life changing language patterns.

I've seen patients stuck in disabling dysfunctions achieve
outstanding objective improvements in their health through practising
these very considerate and careful suggestions.

I hope the importance of this innovative approach to medical health
will spread rapidly to the practice of medicine and to all who need it. I
feel we are in dire need of it."

Dr Susy Mikkelsen, MD, Dip Musculo Skeletal Medicine

"This timely and important book teaches us the language of health. It
explores a practical approach to the philosophy of salutogenics,
teaching the reader how to think in a way that helps their health.

Phil Parker's book is, contrary to most works on language and its
effect on health, easy to read and understand, and incredibly useful.
Phil Parker offers us a way of thinking that will lead to positive
changes in our consciousness and lead to constructive actions to
free patients (and in fact any reader) of the unhealthy burden of
certain hidden but destructive ways of thinking. The way he explains
the effect on language on our life and, especially, the life of a
suffering person, is very clear and I think very useful for the patient."

Dr Jens Torning, GP and Psychotherapist

Phil Parker
DO Dip E Hyp P NLP MBIH Certified Master Practitioner
of NLP

Phil Parker is an internationally renowned lecturer, therapist and innovator in the field of personal development. He has also changed the lives of thousands of people by designing the groundbreaking Lightning Process® seminars.

His core principle is that people are geniuses with amazing skills, qualities and talents, and he hopes he can help as many people as possible to find that out about themselves.

One of Phil's core developments is to introduce a whole new way of thinking about problems and solutions which has required the creation of the new verb 'dû'. The usage of this new concept and word is already rapidly spreading throughout the world, and Phil's vision for it is for it to eventually become part of everyone's everyday language.

Phil has created a wide range of books and audio programmes which have helped many individuals conquer stress, anxiety and panic attacks, sleep issues, weight issues and enhance their personal and professional effectiveness. His work has been translated into a number of languages.

Phil divides his time between his work, family, big motorbikes and loud rock music.

Follow the world of dû by going to www.duing.org

Dû – Unlock your full potential with a word

Phil Parker

Do Dip E Hyp Psyc CMPNLP

Nipton Publishing

NIPTON PUBLISHING
River Plate House, 7-11 Finsbury Circus, London EC2M 7DH

First published in 2011 by Nipton Publishing

A CIP catalogue record for this book is available from the
British Library.

ISBN 978-0-9556482-5-0

Printed in the UK
Cover design by Mulberry Advertising

Acknowledgements

There are so many people to thank that are behind this book, as it has taken over ten years to go from an idea to the object you are now holding. Thanks to all my inspirational teachers, those I found in formal education, in my clients and in my great friends.

Thanks to my amazing support team - Fiona, Helen, Lyds, Ellie and Gary.

Thanks to my very special friends, my family and my kids; Callum, Bethy, Sienna, Mo and Indi who, maybe by having less to unlearn than us adults, seemed to grasp the ideas in this book instantly; "Yeah of course, dad! Duh!" and for the smiles, pancakes and dancing.

And thanks to all those who continue to bring possibility, love and laughter into the world.

Contents

This Book's History

During the course of writing this book it's had many working titles ranging from 'The book of dûing', 'Language - the rocket fuel of change' and 'On the stroke of midnight' to the final decision you see on the cover.

'On the stroke of midnight' came a very close second, as it so nicely conjures up both the changing of the date, year or millennium, as well as that moment in fairy tales when everything shifts; the carriage becomes a pumpkin again, the dress turns back to rags. And yet in the fairy tales not everything does return to as it was before; Cinderella's glass slippers for example stay changed, but even more importantly, once the new way of how the world could be is glimpsed, it can never be seen in the same way again.

You will hear echoes of this in the fairy tale woven through the book.

1. Beginnings

Once upon a time there were three little piggies; the cleverest, brightest eyed piggies you ever did see; all day long they snuffled and oinked happily, as they dug for acorns and truffles in the sunshine - until one Wednesday, at the height of summer, just on the stroke of midnight...

How to use this book

This book has been designed to be a practical guide to making your life better using the ideas and tools that it presents. In order to get the most from the book I recommend that you work through the suggested exercises as you go through it, although if you're anything like me, you'll skip these bits and come back to them later, kicking yourself for not doing it in the suggested order in the first place!

In this book you will find a few words of jargon, like 'Language Pattern'. I will explain each technical word as

1

it occurs in the book to help you become more familiar with them. I have also included a glossary of terms at the back of the book to help with this.

What's it about?

I hope you will find this book as intriguing to read as it has been to write. Inside you'll find a practical approach and an in-depth consideration of three main themes:

- Discovering that the way we use our words is the secret to changing our future for the better
- Looking at the world, and the nature of reality, in a completely new way
- Considering a new and life changing philosophy

Apologies - although I used the '*ph*' word, philosophy, so early in the book, please don't run screaming from the book shop where you're hiding from the rain or killing time before meeting a friend, quite yet. In my experience books about philosophy and language and the nature of reality are usually exceedingly dull and impenetrable, however I hope this book will be quite different. I hope it will be something that easily makes sense and can be applied immediately to the way you think, to rapidly improve your life and future.

As with any discussion involving a philosophy, it will evoke one of a series of possible responses. You may feel these concepts are something you have a degree of fluency with already and embrace them further. Or maybe you might initially be quite surprised by the newness and unfamiliarly of this approach. Or you may even possibly feel outraged by some of the ideas presented, as on first reading they can appear quite challenging.

I hope that wherever you begin from you will be able to appreciate that the purpose of presenting these ideas is not to threaten anyone's world view, but to open the possibility of seeing things in a different way, so that if you ever find yourself stuck and decide that your current approach isn't delivering the solutions that you deserve, you will have another way to consider your options and maybe find a way through.

This book and the Phil Parker Lightning Process (LP), Phil Parker Peak Performance (P4) and other programmes

As the designer of the LP, P4 and a number of other life changing programmes, there are bound to be some of you reading this because you have an interest in these. Others may not have come across the LP, P4 or my work in general, yet, so I'll include a very brief summary of these two programmes.

The LP is a profoundly transformational personal development programme. Run over three days, it is designed to help people make important and vital changes to their lives and health.

There is much literature about the LP but very little detailed information of the contents of the training programme. There are a number of reasons for this:

Firstly some of the core concepts presented in the seminar can initially seem quite challenging and complex. The seminar has been designed to allow for adequate and extensive discussion of these concepts, so that the participants have a good and full understanding of them - but this makes it difficult to produce any brief synopsis that summarises the seminar contents effectively.

Secondly the LP is partly a personal journey, where some of its elements are best discovered whilst being guided and supported by a trained professional - a journey, which again, is very difficult to replicate and manage through just reading about those concepts.

The P4 programme is a two-day intensive change programme developed especially for peak performers in all fields, including business executives, creatives, sports performers, and extreme atheletes and explorers. It trains people in how to achieve un-precedented levels of success in all areas of their lives and work. It too is an interactive training, which packs in a wealth of information and ground-breaking, easily implemented tools into a very short period of time.

So this book is not a 'how to do a Phil Parker seminar at home' book. To get the full benefit of one of those seminars you will need to attend one. It does for the first time, however explore some of the core concepts that drive and are an essential part of the LP, P4 and the other related programmes that I have designed.

This book also provides the right kind of forum for introducing these complex concepts. It should provide an opportunity to explore, explain and discuss them in a deep enough way that most readers will come away with a good enough understanding of what this philosophical approach is and how to use it practically in their lives.

What if?
Philosophy, by its nature, is a best guess, or a model of how things might be, and although most philosophies start out as that, as time passes and they become more familiar and accepted, they begin to be seen as

something quite different. They begin to be thought of as 'the truth', however as Nietzsche rather caustically stated

> *"All things are subject to interpretation whichever interpretation prevails at a given time is a function of power and not truth."*

The philosophical approach of this book is quite new, it doesn't have a long history or massive acceptance within humankind, so let's begin from the premise that maybe nothing in this book is really true. For some of you that might be a bit of a relief, as that perspective frees us up from having to either accept everything, or to challenge everything within these pages; instead treat this as just a discussion, a chat in the philosophical bar of life.

So if we don't have to accept any of the contents of this book as a truth, then what is the best way to approach it? My experience is that the most effective way to consider the ideas presented is not to ask, "Is this true or false?" but to ask instead, "What would happen and what would be different if it were this way?"

This approach has interestingly been behind some of the most radical advances in science which the noted scientific historian Thomas Kuhn has called 'paradigm' shifts (Kuhn, 1962). A paradigm (pronounced *para-dime*) is the word used to describe an idea that has become so familiar and accepted by experts that it becomes **the** explanation of the way something is. An example would be the idea that gravity is responsible for causing an object to fall when you let go of it. Kuhn describes a paradigm shift to be when the whole of a completely accepted concept and all the implications that come from it becomes obsolete. So if we were to discover that it was not in fact gravity that made objects fall but the downwards flight of billions of flying microscopic bacteria (it isn't) that was really responsible for the movements of the falling objects then we would have to reassess many other things that were based around our idea of gravity and its effects.

Radical advances and paradigm shifts occur when sufficient evidence comes to light to suggest that the current prevailing view (the best guess that has become the accepted truth) no longer fits the documented facts.

Science is riddled which such shifts, a famous example is the shift in ideas of what was at the centre of the universe. From at least the 1st century the Ptolemaic model of the universe (named after Ptolemy, a brilliant Greco-Roman living in A.D. 90) was the accepted truth. It stated that the earth was the centre of the universe and everything rotated around **it**. It took fourteen more centuries, and quite a period of transition to shift to the current Copernican model (named after Nicolaus Copernicus, 1473-1543). In this model the earth is considered to rotate around the sun and the sun is considered to be centre of the solar system, but neither are considered to be the centre of the universe.

The previous version of truth seems, historically, to cling on for as long as it possibly can, desperately avoiding extinction or change with the resilience and tenacity of a drowning man clinging to a sodden, sinking log.

Eventually it is finally replaced by the newer model which often, within a generation or two, becomes the new truth, and the cycle begins again.

> *"A new scientific truth does not triumph by convincing its opponents and making them see the*

light, but rather because its opponents eventually die, and a new generation grows up that is familiar with it." Max Planck (Nobel prize winning physicist)

So, my hope for this book and ideas within it are that they encourage you to make a small shift, a major shift or a paradigm shift in your world view that gives you a better chance of a happy and fulfilled life. Certainly thousands of others who I've presented these concepts to have done just that. I also hope that the ideas presented here are never taken as a truth, as the transition to that state tends to cause stagnation, righteousness and conflict. I would rather that they continued to be considered as a set of possibilities, albeit very powerful, empowering and life affirming ones.

So, why all this focus on science, philosophy and the nature of reality? Well, in this book we are going to go on a, hopefully, exciting journey of exploring what we think of as reality. And that's pretty important because all our decisions, choices and judgements, whether brilliant or disastrous, are based on what **we** think is real.

The journey begins by looking at one of the most important and often overlooked influences of success and disaster in our lives – language.

2. Talking Yourself Into Trouble

.. *for on that Wednesday night, just on the stroke of midnight, one of the piggies woke up with a start and realised that something was very different. He sniffed the air, and there was no denying it - the beautiful scent of the Enchanted Acorn was drifting on the breeze. Legend had it, as every young piggy in the world knew, that a piggy could find the secret of contentment once they dug up the Enchanted Acorn. The piggy woke up his friends, but even before they stretched, yawned and grumpily rubbed their eyes, the scent had disappeared, like mist in a forest.*

Maybe, they suggested, the piggy had been dreaming, maybe he should stop thinking about the Enchanted Acorn and that fairy story for babies, and maybe he should eat less cheese before bed and keep his late night delusions to himself...

Having spent years listening to people talk, both in everyday conversation and in therapeutic situations, I was consistently amazed at how much of what people say was either a vast and unpleasant distortion of reality or made the world a much more difficult place for them to live or be happy in. It appeared that people were unwittingly spending a lot of time *talking themselves into trouble*.

And often, it seemed, when people weren't talking in this way they were thinking it.

Of course it would be wrong to generalise and claim that this applies to all people all of the time but in my experience it was just far too common.

The focus of this book then is to explore and address some of the commonest types of troublesome language, and the first of these is the use of the 'Negative Want'.

The Negative Want
The Negative Want is such an important pattern to notice and change. It shows up in so many places, each time preventing life from being exciting, vital and fulfilling - spotting and dealing with them is an essential skill for getting a life you love. Spotting Negative Wants becomes even more useful when used in combination with the other main concepts we will be covering in later chapters.

It is easy to spot, as it classically shows up when someone expresses a desire for something, but instead of saying what they want, they say what they don't want. Consider the following example:

Barman: "What do you want to drink, sir?"

Customer: "Oh, not beer please."

Barman: "Excellent. So you don't want beer. What do you want?"

Customer: "And tonight I don't feel like a gin and tonic."

Barman: "Very good sir, but what do you want?"

Customer: "I don't think I'll have a red glass of wine from the fine vines of the Napa Valley."

Barman: "Good. But please tell me what you want?"

Customer: "I don't think I'll have a…"

And so on.

Although you might be quite surprised if someone operated like this whilst ordering drinks in a bar, it is actually very common to hear people answering questions about what they want with an almost endless collection of Negative Want's - just listen out for them and you'll start to find this trait everywhere.

In this apparently extreme example we can see that not saying what you want has at least a few disastrous consequences, namely not getting what you want and others starting to become less patient with you or starting to avoid you. In addition to that minor inconvenience there is another more sinister effect, which is all to do with the way the brain works.

The Brain and Negatives

To understand the effect of Negative Wants on the brain, notice what happens when you work through the following simple exercise.

Exercise 2.1

For the next three seconds follow this instruction.

"Try not to think of the President of the USA, and don't think of him juggling twelve purple monkeys!"

Notice what happened when you tried to not think of it… you would have found that, at least initially, you just couldn't stop thinking about it.

This is because of the way the brain works. The brain processes these instructions by firstly considering all the elements of the instruction. In this case there are three major components of the instruction:

1. To avoid thinking about the two following things:
2. The 'President of the USA'
3. And 'him juggling twelve purple monkeys'

Clearly by step two we've already done the exact opposite of what we have been instructed to do just in an attempt to understand the instruction. This is why the brain just can't effectively process negative phrases like the one above without first thinking about what it's not supposed to think of.

It is a bit like sunbathing on a beach and noticing a sign, at a short distance out to sea, poking out of the water. Because the sign is difficult to read from that distance you might swim over to see what it says and when you get there it says "Danger Sharks, No Swimming!"

Alternatively if someone is nervous about a job interview and you are trying to help him or her to be better prepared and calmer you might helpfully ask, "What do you want to feel in the interview?" If they reply, which they usually will, "Not so nervous and stressed, not to have that stomach churning, sicky feeling", then you can probably already guess what their brain immediately thinks about as they say this (nervous, stressed, stomach churning and sicky feeling). Obviously this is not the kind of thing that you wish them to be thinking about, but you are too late, they were, unfortunately, just too quick at thinking about exactly the wrong things, and now, in spite of your good intentions, will be feeling even worse.

It can be really valuable to become more aware of your language, noticing the way you talk to others and especially the way you talk to yourself (yes, everyone does talk to themselves and it's not a sign of madness!) In doing this you will start to avoid these neurological dead-ends that just make life more difficult.

Exercise 2.2
This exercise is designed to help you to recognise Negative Wants by presenting common examples. Once you've recognised the presence of the Negative Wants you can quickly identify how the Negative Want forces your brain to think of exactly the wrong kind of things. Consider these examples:

1. "Children, I don't want you to shout at each other again."

   The instruction that the children's brains hears is:

   "Shout at each other again"

2. This one is a classic from doctor's and dentist's surgeries around the world.

   "I am going to inject you with a needle, it's not very big, don't be scared, it won't hurt very much."

   What the brain actually hears is:

   "I am going to inject you with a needle" "it's very big" "be scared" "hurt very much"

3. "Don't be nervous."

   The instruction the brain hears is:

   "Be nervous"

4. "I want to be unstressed, not worry and be care[1]-free."

   This seems like a lovely thing to wish for someone, but a quick evaluation of it will show that the instruction the brain hears is:

   "Be stressed, worry and have cares[1]"

---

[1] In this sentence the usage of the word care means worries.

5. "Don't get dizzy whilst walking along that dangerously high wall and don't fall off."

What the brain actually hears is:

"Get dizzy" a reminder of how **high and dangerous** the wall is and **"fall off"**

Notice how in each example the person has achieved exactly the opposite of what they wanted by using the Negative Want.

Exercise 2.3
Now use the following examples to practise spotting the Negative Wants:

"I don't want to think about how crowded it is in here."

"I want to believe I am not going to get it wrong again."

"I am not going to get stressed."

"I tell myself this is not going to be too difficult."

"I am going to resist eating that cake."

"I do not want chocolate."

"I do not want to hate the gym."

"I am not going to go to pieces when I give the presentation."

Answers

"I don't want to think about how <u>crowded</u> it is <u>in here</u>."

"I want to believe <u>I am</u> not <u>going to get it wrong again</u>."

"<u>I am</u> not <u>going to get stressed</u>."

"<u>I tell myself this is</u> not <u>going to be too difficult</u>."

"<u>I am going to</u> resist <u>eating that cake</u>."

"<u>I do</u> not <u>want chocolate</u>."

"<u>I do</u> not <u>want to hate the gym</u>."

"<u>I am</u> not <u>going to go to pieces when I give the presentation</u>."

Hidden Negatives

There is one further and brilliantly clever way we have of expressing things as negatives without noticing them, and I call these Hidden Negatives.

Look at the phrases: can you spot the negative?

1. I want to be bold when I deal with this
2. I need to be brave
3. I want to be in control
4. I want to be better
5. I want security
6. I want it to feel safe
7. I want to be free

On the surface these sentences look pretty good, positive and reasonable, but scratch beneath the surface and the problems start to show.

16

The problem is what these good positive words make you think about.

1. **Bold.** If you need to be bold to deal with '*this*', then what kind of a situation are you dealing with? Not a very nice one, it must be something that is quite difficult, challenging or scary. As a result the word 'bold' tends to make people think of those negative things.

2. **Brave.** The situation is very similar to the 'bold statement'. If you need to be brave when facing something, then you must be dealing with something fairly uncomfortable.

3. **Control.** Wanting to be in control sounds quite reasonable, until we pause to consider what kinds of things do we need to be in control of? Things that are going well, are predictable and tend to be reliable? No, on the whole we apply 'control' to those things that are dangerous, chaotic and are likely to get out of hand; things like crowds, traffic or dangerous dogs, etc. So when we think of the word 'control' it naturally conjures up ideas of chaos and danger because that's when we need to use control.

4. **Better.** Again this sounds like a good thing to want, but it instantly makes us ask the question "better than what?" and as soon as we do that we find ourselves thinking about the very thing we want to not have again.

5. 6. and 7. **Security, Safety and Freedom.** These are three of the most commonly wished for things - security, safety and freedom. Again on the face of it

they seem quite reasonable things to want, but like 'control' they have a darker side to them. The normal usage of the words contains a sense of getting away from something, as in:
- Safe from something
- Secure from something
- Free[2] from something

And as a result they are tainted with this idea and like the other examples in this section encourage the brain to think about the Hidden Negatives, precisely the things you don't want to be thinking about.

Exercise 2.4
Make a list today of everything you say or think or anything you hear someone else saying that is full of Negative Wants or Hidden Negatives. Note down what was said and then quickly work out what you or they have actually told the brain to do. If it was you that was using these negatives then ask yourself "is that really what you want your brain to be focusing on?"

If not then create a replacement statement that only includes what you want.

Health Wants
If you've tried the exercise above you might have been quite surprised at how difficult and unfamiliar it was to state things in a positive way. In my experience one of the trickiest areas for people to use positive words and wants rather than Negative Wants is in the area of health.

---

[2] Although 'free' is not always referring to a negative - as it can sometimes mean absolute, complete and peaceful freedom - but that is a different experience to this concept of 'free from something'.

Exercise 2.5

Consider the statements below:

"I want my back to not hurt and be stiff."

"I want to not have this headache."

"I want my legs to feel pain free."

Clearly you can now spot the Negative Wants, but can you change them into positive ones?

Using the first example of "I want my back to not hurt and be stiff", I've found that when most people try to change it into a positive, it sounds something like this:

Change 1: "I want my back to be less painful and not as tight."

But again we can notice although these are different words, they are still Negative Wants.

Change 2: "I want a pain free back and for it not to seize up."

Again we've run into the same problem.

Change 3: "I want my back to be better."

This sounds good but 'better' is a Hidden Negative. As soon as you say 'better' your brain wants to know what you are comparing it too and asks "better than what?" the answer is "better than the amount of pain and stiffness I have right now" and once again we are in negatives.

19

s surprising how difficult it is to complete such a simple exercise.

To help you out I've provided a short list below of some of the kinds of words that can be used for Positive Wants about physical issues:

Well, healthy, comfortable, fit, vital, soft, warm, cool, relaxed, energised, easy, flexible, fluid, supple, strong, etc.

Once people read the example words above, it all suddenly seems so simple, and they are amazed and curious as to why they found it so challenging to complete the exercise.

What is very interesting is that it seems that we have an enormous, easily accessible library of words to describe illness and poor health, but relatively few words, which we have to search quite hard to find, to describe how something is when it is working well. This is probably because we are relatively unaware and uninterested in our bodies when they are working fine and pay very little attention to them when they are well. Much of our focus and awareness of our bodies seems to be linked to times when they are not working well. It's in those times that we need to describe how our body feels to others and so that's when we build up our library of words that describe our body, as we start to think of words to explain what is going on inside us. The more we do this the more dominant and familiar those words will become when talking about our bodies and health; as we can see from our understanding of Negative Wants on the way the brain works, this is not generally a good thing.

Wellness and Disease Scales

In medical research it's important to collect detailed information about any new treatment or approach to find out if it is useful or not. However there are a number of issues specific to humans, which make analysing this kind of data especially complex. One of these is the effect of negative language. In my research team's detailed enquiries into creating useful research protocols we have found one major difficulty. Based on your understanding of the previous section, can you identify what the problem is from these examples taken from currently used and well-respected research questionnaires?

From the Self Efficacy Scale used for clients with chronic fatigue. Clients can select a score between 1 and 10 where 1 is not at all confident and 10 is very confident. This all seems good so far…

Just for clarity let me point out that in this case I haven't added any additional bolding of the text or underlining. So all the bolding and underlining you see below is exactly as it is on the standard form handed out to patients.

> "How confident are you that you can keep the **<u>fatigue</u>** caused by your disease from interfering with the things you want to do?"

> "How confident are you that you can keep the **<u>physical discomfort</u>** or **<u>pain</u>** of your disease from interfering with the things you want to do?"

> "How confident are you that you can keep the **<u>emotional distress</u>** caused by your disease from interfering with the things you want to do?"

Now you should be able to see the questions on these forms in a very different light. I am certain that whoever designed them designed them with good intention to help measure people's current health state so that changes could be recorded and measured, with a view to finding good treatment options for future clients. But without the knowledge presented in this chapter you can see how easy it is to unintentionally create problems with the data collected, and to influence how the clients feel as a result of filling in those forms.

If we now bold and underline all the parts of the statements that focus on the negatives, it starts to read like an instruction manual for how to get ill. Now read through the same form just saying the bold/underlined sections.

> "How confident are you that **you can keep the fatigue** caused by **your disease** from **interfering with the things you want to do**?"

This instructs the reader to keep their fatigue, to think about their disease and how much it will interfere with their life.

> "How confident are you that **you can keep the physical discomfort or pain of your disease** from **interfering with the things you want to do**?"

This tells them to keep their physical discomfort and pain and to focus on their continuing disease and how much it will interfere with their life.

> "How confident are you that **you can keep the emotional distress** caused by **your disease** from **interfering with the things you want to do**?"

And this one asks them to think about their emotional distress as well as reminding them again to think of their disease and how much it interferes with their life.

In addition to the massive amount of negatives here in this particular questionnaire there are also some very powerfully Closed Questions. A Closed Question only has a limited number of possible responses to it.

An example would be:

Do you own any shoes?

The answer would be yes or no.

This is a relatively clean question, but some are a bit more problematic:

"Would you like to go to bed with or without a bath?"

The answer would be with or without; but, as every parent who has used this type of approach knows, independent of whether a bath is chosen or not, the child has implicitly agreed to the fact that 'going to bed' is not an option and that will it occur in the very near future.

The question,

> "How confident are you that you can keep the **fatigue** caused by your disease from interfering with the things you want to do?"

is also closed, in that certain responses are allowed and other things are predetermined.

Based on the question, do they have a choice as to whether they will continue to have their disease or not?

Again based on this question, do they have a choice as to whether they will continue to have their fatigue or not?

There is also an implication that their disease and its fatigue will also interfere, to one degree or another, with the things they want to do.

Similar to the bath and bed scenario, in which the child's choices were limited to bath and bed or just bed, the only thing that is up for debate is whether they will have:

Disease plus fatigue and lots of difficulty carrying on with the things they want to do

Or

Disease plus fatigue and little difficulty carrying on with the things they want to do

The idea that they will definitely continue to have the disease and the fatigue is stated as a fact and the idea of 'not having the disease and fatigue' is just not an option.

Unfortunately my research team and I have found that these kind of language problems are present to one degree or another in most of the common and well respected scales and score charts that are currently used to assess change in clients. This is not done through malice, but just because it's not really considered as a factor that could really have any influence on the patient's physical health - but both my experience and that of others (Richter, Eck, Straube, Miltner, & Weiss, 2010) suggests that it does. We will be covering this later this in more detail.

Hidden Traps

These negative ways of speaking were one of the key problems I noticed cropping up in people's conversations which kept their lives stuck - and now that you understand the concepts of Negative Wants and the effect they have on the brain, you will find they are fairly easy to spot and to change. However, I also started to notice another more subtle way of 'talking yourself into trouble' that seemed to cause even more problems - and due to its subtlety and widespread occurrence it seemed to be even more difficult for the individual to notice than Negative Wants. Like the widespread usage of the cancer causing asbestos as a standard housing material between 1945-85, the difficulty with trying to deal with anything that is harmful to you, whilst being unaware of any risk, is that until you realise what is going on any change is unlikely.

Identifying these subtle problems was therefore very exciting. It didn't take rocket science to work out that if I had been able to notice these ways of speaking, then it should be relatively easy to teach others to notice them and for them to then change those ways of speaking.

Consider the following statements. They are exactly the kind of statements that you will find nestling comfortably and apparently appropriately in a number of the conversations that you will hear today.

1. "This kind of cold and cloudy weather gets me down."
2. "My boss was really angry and made me upset again today."
3. "I would have been on time but the traffic made me late."

They are not Negative Wants and on first glance they may all seem quite reasonable and not that problematic as statements. However in order to understand these seemingly innocuous statements in a new light I'd like to introduce you to one of the core concepts of this book, Language Patterns.

3. Life Changing Language Patterns

...he tried to snuggle back down to sleep but a small whisper of a voice seemed to keep jolting him out of his sleepiness. Following the sound he trotted out of the door and into the dark, dark forest night.

The sound became clearer as he entered the very deepest part of the forest, he could make it out more now, the tiny voice spoke with a certain kind of a rhythm, and it sounded eversomuch like someone practising spells...

In the previous chapter I introduced the idea of troublesome language and its two major components, Negative Wants, and the other more hidden component Language Patterns.

Language Patterns are something that I've been developing and working with for over a decade. It's a new approach to helping people rapidly make massive changes in their lives and it's based around a relatively simple yet vitally important concept. It allows you to rapidly work out if what you've said or thought is really accurate and factual, or if there is a more useful way to put it.

Rather surprisingly this simple attention to the way you use language has already changed thousands of people's lives for the better. This chapter begins our exploration into the importance that language has in changing your life.

The term 'Language Pattern' is described in the glossary; in this context it means a particular way of speaking or using language, and throughout the book we will be exploring how we use language and why we should pay more attention to it.

Can language be that important?
Yes it really can. To understand why it's so important I would like you to consider that our language is a bit like a computer screen for the mind. The screen is not the computer, but it is the easiest way to find out what's going on inside it.

Conscious and Unconscious
For the purpose of this discussion, I'd also like to introduce the ideas of the conscious and unconscious parts of the mind. In this book the 'conscious mind' means the part of us that actively chooses something. Deciding to have a coffee or an orange juice at a restaurant would be a conscious decision.

In this book 'the unconscious' refers to the choices and decisions that are not the result of conscious activity, or necessarily having rationally considered all the options, an example might be someone who was scared of horses or someone who is unconfident amongst unfamiliar people. Unconscious decisions and

28

behaviours are often the result of some old understanding that we have about how the world works, which was created by us, for good reasons, as a response to some event in the past. These unconscious processes may or may not have become out-dated, and independent of whether they are still up to date and accurate or not they continue to exert a very powerful influence on the way we think and act, as they are our version of what is true and what reality is.

How do we speak?
Millions of thought processes go on every second inside our head resulting in our thoughts, ideas and actions. The way we form, understand and communicate these thought processes is with our words and language. Language can be considered to consist of two major parts, what we say (the content) and how we say it (the structure - the precise words we use, their order and grammar, etc). Consider this example:

"I think I will have a banana and cheese sandwich."

In that sentence the *content* is about your desire for a weird sandwich and the *structure* is which words are chosen and in what order, etc.

But if you pause for a minute and consider the question, 'How do we actually construct sentences and chose the words to fit what we mean?' then mostly the answer is, 'We don't'. Well not consciously anyway.

In the example above, why did we put the words in that order? Why did we say 'banana and cheese' and not 'cheese and banana'? Are we imagining one is put into the sandwich first, one is more important, one is on top of the other, that it sounds better to our ears in that way, or we've unconsciously alphabetised it? There must be some reason for us choosing to say banana before cheese, but we probably won't know what that reason is *consciously*.

We build the sentence by first of all having the thoughts/the content (*banana and cheese sandwich*) and then some kind of magical 'black box' process occurs which seems to 'just' create the sentences, the word order, the grammar and all its component parts for us.

And that is what makes language so interesting - clearly it's not our conscious mind that is choosing the sentence structure, yet we are choosing it; therefore it must be chosen by the more unconscious, more automatic part of our mind.

If the words are chosen by that more unconscious part of our mind, then examining the sentence structure gives us a real window into to the mind and particularly what we think about the way the world is. Looking at the structure of our language therefore is one of the best ways to understand our version of 'reality'. It gives us a direct way of examining how the unconscious mind sees the world and what rules it thinks the world operates by.

Clearly if we wish to change how we relate to the world for the better it would be good to start by recognising where we are not relating to it very usefully. This suddenly elevates the importance of paying close attention to how we use language from being a fairly arcane academic pursuit to being something of immense significance.

Now that I've introduced the idea that language might be a more important subject to focus on than you previously might have thought, I'd like to turn the focus onto one of the key elements of the Language Patterns, the Passive Perspective.

4. Passive Perspective

...rounding a huge gnarled tree, he stumbled upon a tiny, brightly coloured elf, who seeming as surprised as he, stepped back in shock, and as she did so she became tangled up into a huge spider's web. The more she wriggled the more she became stuck fast...

Understanding the Passive Perspective is vital to working with Language Patterns, and, as you will shortly discover, making your life great.

Let's begin by explaining what I mean by the Passive Perspective, and although it's a fairly long phrase (and covered in the Glossary) it's thankfully fairly easy to understand.

If someone is describing a situation that was:

1. Beyond their control
2. Not within their power to influence
3. Nothing they could do anything about
4. When they had no options
5. When they were a victim[3] of circumstance

---

[3] Please note: the word victim is not used here in the judgemental sense that it sometimes has in popular psychology, as in "she's just being a victim".

then the Passive Perspective is being used. And the statements they make when talking about such things in this way I have called 'Passive Statements'.

Examples are:
It was raining on my holiday.

The car hit me when I was walking on the pavement.

In these statements, we can notice the Passive Perspective; where the events are simply not within your control. For example there isn't much you can do about the rain or the car that hit you. As a result you are passive in your relationship to them.

These Passive Statements are an appropriate usage of the Passive Perspective; we can all recognise events and situations where we are completely unable to control things - the weather and other people's driving are two good examples.

Exercise 4.1
Using the list in the Passive Perspective section above identify which sentences are passive.

1. I was unfortunate enough to be hit by a drunk driver.
2. I chose to wear these shoes because I like them.
3. They cancelled my flight and there wasn't another one until the next morning.
4. I don't go to that bar often.
5. The town flooded because of an unusual amount of rain.

To increase your understanding of this important topic I have outlined an explanation of why each one was an example of the Passive Perspective or not.

1. I was unfortunate enough to be hit by a drunk driver.

Passive. There was really nothing they could do anything about the drunk driver hitting them.

2. I chose to wear these shoes because I like them.

Not passive. They had options about which shoes they wore and they chose these ones.

3. They cancelled my flight and there wasn't another one until the next morning.

Passive. The flight being cancelled was beyond their control, and they couldn't control when the next one was due either.

4. I don't go to that bar often.

Not passive. They have options as to which bar they go to and most of the time they don't go to that one.

5. The town flooded because of an unusual amount of rain.

Passive. The unusual amount of rain that caused the flooding was not within their control; the people of the town were victims of circumstance.

The Passive Problem
This all seems fine so far, however, you may have already noticed that there is unfortunately one major problem with the use of the Passive Perspective. This problem is:

- The Passive Perspective identifies a situation as being something that we can't do much about.

- But sometimes it is possible to say or think that we are completely unable to influence something, when actually we are completely mistaken and are able to have a massive influence on it.

I call this misuse of the Passive Perspective and Passive Statements as using 'Passive Language'.

Even with this basic introduction to the idea of Passive Language you can instantly see the negative consequences of using it.

Imagine we find ourselves in a difficult situation, where it seems that we are unable to do anything about what's happening. But unfortunately we are wrong - we can do something about it. The belief that we are powerless in this situation will naturally prevent us from even trying to make the situation better. This is because we assume that we just can't make a difference, even though in reality we could do something to influence the situation for the better.

We will be covering Passive Language in much more detail in the next few chapters - including how to spot it and the disastrous consequences it can have on people's lives. But the first step is to be able to distinguish the correct use of the Passive Perspective from its misuse. The key to this is getting familiar with three very important concepts *Influence, Factual Accuracy* and *Opinions.*

5. Fact and Fiction

... "Help, help, there is no way out!" she yelled, rousing a sleeping shape who moved slowly and ominously towards her...

In the preceding chapters I have already highlighted the need to become skilled at considering what we say and what we think. We've explored how people talk themselves into trouble with Negatives Wants and the additional hidden problems called Language Patterns. We've started to understand the Passive Perspective, Passive Statements and their misuse 'Passive Language', and how we need to be certain that the things that are stated as being out of our control are really out of our control. This chapter explores ideas and tools useful for making this judgement, and begins by looking at a vital concept that forms the basis of much of my work, the idea of *influence.*

Influence

Looking this word up in the dictionary will give quite a confused list of definitions, ranging from the magical effects that stars were historically thought to have on people to the one we will be using in this book; the idea of being able to have an effect on some object or situation.

It's important to note that this concept differs from a number of other related terms such as:

- Blame
- Fault
- Responsibility

The difference being that 'influence' looks beyond who or what was to blame or at fault, and instead looks at what could be done to make things change.

So 'having an influence' means being someone who is going to do something about resolving a situation, by recognising the elements they can influence and then affecting those things to make a difference.

I often tell the following story about a bus journey to emphasise this important point.

Imagine we are on a bus, and whilst driving at speed down the road the bus driver suddenly falls into a coma and slumps over the wheel. This coma is because he is an insulin dependent diabetic and he hasn't taken his medication or eaten that day, so his blood sugar levels have dropped to dangerous levels. Who is to blame and at fault for this situation?

Since the bus driver is in charge of monitoring and managing his blood sugar levels properly so that he is competent to drive safely, and he hasn't done that we could reasonably say that he is at fault for the situation that we, the passengers, now find ourselves in. His blood sugar levels aren't something we can influence, so they are things that we are 'passive' to.

But who has an influence in potentially recovering the situation, for making it good and saving everyone?

The answer is, of course, anyone who can get to the wheel in time and take over the driving.

We could, of course, spend the remaining seconds of our life blaming the bus driver as we head towards the oncoming traffic, but maybe there's more value in letting go of the idea of finding someone, or something, to blame and instead use that time more purposefully to rescue the situation.

So to summarise, the concept of influence that I want to use, and for you to work with, throughout this book is not about fault finding, and not even about thinking "I should have influenced that situation differently" (because that is just blaming yourself and of no use). Instead it's all about asking "What can I do about a situation to make it good or better?"

Let's consider these three statements:

1. "This kind of cold and cloudy weather gets me down."
2. "My boss was really angry and made me upset again today."
3. "I would have been on time but the traffic made me late."

In all of the above issues there are things that are fairly unchangeable:

1. The weather
2. The boss
3. The traffic

But we can also notice there are other events appearing in the statements:

1. The down feelings
2. The upset feelings
3. The lateness

These things appear, from the way the sentence is constructed, to be linked, and are dependent on or caused by these unchangeable things.

Instead let's consider it in a different light. We know there are some things that are unavailable for change (weather, boss, traffic), so if we want change to occur and the problem to be resolved we need to look at everything else involved in the problem, and the bad and the good news is, the main thing left to change is you.

This is 'bad' as it means we can no longer try to shift the blame onto other people or external things for the way things are, or to try and shift the responsibility for sorting things out onto them either. It also means we can no longer pretend that there's nothing to be done about the situation.

Equally it is 'good' in that the person who needs to do something about resolving the issue is someone we have great influence over, ourselves.

This shift is one of the core themes that you will find running throughout the rest of the book.

Factual Accuracy

Now that we have a good understanding of the Passive Perspective and Influence it's time to start to use these ideas to examine our thoughts and words for accuracy.

Once again we'll use our three example statements. In the section on the Passive Perspective there was a list that helped us to identify if a statement was passive. Here it is again as a reminder. This time we will consider if the examples meet the requirements on the list, or not.

Passive Statement List
1. Beyond their control
2. Not within their power to influence
3. Nothing they could do anything about
4. When they had no options
5. When they were a victim of circumstance

Statements to check for accuracy:
1) "This kind of cold and cloudy weather gets me down."
2) "My boss was really angry and made me upset again today."
3) "I would have been on time but the traffic made me late."

Statement 1: "This kind of cold and cloudy weather **gets me down.**"

Remember we are not challenging the accuracy of the fact the weather is beyond their control, we know that it is, we are checking the accuracy of the other part of the statement "the cold and cloudy weather gets me down".

Let's apply the criteria from the Passive Statement list to see how accurate the statement is:

1. Control: Is it really beyond their control to 'get down' - does that have to happen *because* the weather is cold and cloudy?

2. Power: Do they really have no power over how they feel about it?

3. Nothing they could do: Is there nothing at all they could do to feel better, even if it were cold and cloudy?

41

4. Options: Did they have no option but to feel that way? Was that the only possibility? Do other people seem to have other options in this situation?

5. Victim: Did the weather *make* them down? Was their mood purely due to the circumstances?

Does that happen every single time, if not then the things are not as linked as they have stated them.

Is it possible for them to be ok when the weather is cold and cloudy? What if they were inside and didn't notice the weather, would they still feel down then?

We can see that these questions are all slightly different ways of asking the same thing: 'Is it true that you had no influence (using the meaning discussed earlier) to change the outcome?'

It seems to me that it is very unlikely that this is something that they have absolutely *no* influence over at all. And if they have some influence, even a tiny bit, then they cannot, by definition, be passive to that situation. It also follows that if they have some influence then, although they cannot change the event beyond their control (in this case the weather) they can change the effect of, and their response to, that event.

So we can conclude that they had defined themselves as passive to the weather (which was true) but also as passive to their bad mood (which was not entirely accurate). This misuse of the Passive Perspective ("My mood is something that was totally caused by the weather and nothing to do with me") is a good example of what I have called 'Passive Language'.

Statement 2: "My boss was really angry and made me upset again today"

We can assume that they are being factually accurate as they report their boss' mood, but once again we need to consider the other half of the statement, which is all about their reaction to the boss' anger.

Again let's apply the criteria from the Passive Statement list to see how accurate the statement is:

1. Control: Whilst we can agree that the boss does have a certain degree of control over some things, such as their future at the company, their wages, etc., we also need to ask "Is it really true that their boss has the ability to control their mood?" If this were true, the boss would have had to somehow master the skill of being a human puppeteer, pulling some 'invisible strings' so that he could make people do things, often against their will, anytime he wished to. Clearly this is not accurate at all. The boss is not a magical puppeteer, he could certainly be emotional and manipulative around you, but he is not *in control* of you, or able to make you feel emotions. You do that. Emotions come from within, not from the outside. By this I mean although you might be responding to things outside of you, like your boss, **you** are creating the emotions inside. One of the easiest ways to verify this is to remember a time when you were just thinking about something, like a forthcoming date, interview or doctor's appointment, that hadn't happened yet, but you were excited, worried, stressed or nervous about it. The event has yet to happen, yet you are feeling emotions about it. The person you are meeting on the date, the interviewer, the doctor cannot be

43

causing those emotions in you, as none of those people are there with you at that moment. It must be you that is causing those emotions.

2.   Power: When their boss is angry, is it really true that the employee has absolutely no power over how they feel about it?

3.   Nothing they could do: Is there really nothing at all they could do to feel better, even if the boss were angry?

4.   Options: Did they have no option but to feel that way? Was that the only possibility? Do other people seem to have other options in this situation?

5.   Victim: Did the boss really *make* them upset? Was their mood made to happen just by the boss' actions alone?

Does that happen every single time anyone is angry around them? If not, then the things are not as linked as they have stated them to be.

A few examples might help to explain this further as for many people this concept can be quite unfamiliar and it still seems absolutely true to say, "but he really did make me feel...(insert the appropriate word here, e.g. angry, sad, upset, ugly, etc.)"

Exercise 5.1
How would someone feel if someone else angrily told them that they really hated them?

You might imagine that they would definitely be upset, but actually that is not always true.

For some of you reading you may have had the experience, as an adult, of being around kids. There are times when the child really wants something they can't have, like a sweet or a particular toy, or maybe they want for it to be their birthday today and not in a few months time. The child may respond to this refusal to provide what they wish for with an outburst such as:

"I hate you, I hate you, I hate you."

And if they are a teenager it maybe something even stronger!

Most parents will recognise that although the child is genuinely angry, or the teenager enraged, there is actually no good reason for you to get upset as they probably don't *really* mean what they are saying. You recognise they are just letting off steam at not getting what they want.

Consider politicians who clash angrily in a public debate over an issue and then meet up for a chat and a drink afterwards, because although politically they are rivals, personally they are close friends.

Sports-people such as footballers and others, often show a similar set of behaviours. Sometimes filled with such raw competitiveness during a match that it wouldn't look out of place in a bar room brawl. Yet after the match, or when they join a team representing their country, they now naturally consider these same men who are their weekly on-pitch rivals, to be their closest friends.

So, on reflection, it seems that there are many places and occasions where it is quite natural to be able to be around 'people being angry' such as the children in the example above, and to be quite calm and unaffected by it. And it's also clearly possible to change your relationship to how someone, or something 'makes you feel', as in the example of the political or football rivals.

Again we can see that these questions are all slightly different ways of asking the same question. 'Is it true that you had no influence (using the meaning discussed earlier) to change how angry you felt?' and again the answer is, 'No, it's not true, if other people can deal with this in a different way then, it is possible to deal with it differently'.

Exercise 5.2
Finally, imagine if you saw one person, Sam, hit another person, Joe, very hard on the back. How would Joe, who has just been hit, feel?

You might imagine that they would feel angry, upset, saddened or enraged. Because everyone knows that when you get hit it makes you angry, upset, saddened, enraged or (add your own version of what emotion you must feel).

But surely there is the possibility:

Scenario 1: That Joe was choking on some food and his friend, Sam, hit him to dislodge food and saved his life. How would Joe feel then at having been hit? He would probably feel very happy and thankful.

Scenario 2: That the hit, which landed on Joe's back, was the final punch in a boxing competition. As the bell rings Joe knows that although that was a hard blow, it was not enough for his opponent to win. He now knows he's survived the bout and has won on points and the final punch tells him he is now World Champion. How does he feel now?

Scenario 3: That Sam is actually Joe's son who has been in a coma for 5 years. How does Joe feel as his son demonstrates his complete recovery and return of strength with this powerful blow to his back?

So we can see the hit itself does not **cause** the emotion, so the emotion is not completely dependent on the event. The emotion is determined by our **response** to the event. The emotion therefore is dependent on **us.**

Equally it's completely valid to recognise that although people can't make you experience emotions, since, as we are now discovering, you are in charge of those, it is also true that people can very much help and assist you to feel emotions. But notice the words:

- Help
- Assist

They still cannot make you feel those emotions unless you are going to go along with them. They are only a secondary player in the development of these emotions - you are the key player. If you decide not to respond to their cues, not to rise to the bait, and to stay calm, then you will.

This does not of course mean we can go around hitting people and then telling them it's their response that is making them angry and not us. That would be a foolish, unpleasant and a pointless application of this concept.

The true purpose of this idea has, I think, never been better or more eloquently summarised than in the Serenity Prayer.

Serenity Prayer
The Serenity Prayer has appeared in a number of different forms throughout its life, but probably the simplest version is:

> *God grant me the serenity to accept the things I cannot change.*
> *The courage, to change the things I can.*
> *And the wisdom, to know the difference.*

When I first came across this three-point guide to life I was struck, as many are, by its simplicity and depth. I imagined it had been around for almost ever, or maybe had been painstakingly written down with quill on parchment by a cloistered medieval monk, but actually it's much younger than that. It makes its earliest recorded appearance as late as 1950, in a sermon by the noted preacher Reinhold Niebuhr (1892-1971), who originally came up with it in the 1930's. It's gained popularity through it's usage in the 12 step/Alcoholics Anonymous programmes and has changed a few times in emphasis on it's journey to the relatively widespread familiarity it now enjoys.

Part of it's beauty is that it barely needs any additional explanation, as its core meaning is abundantly clear: that we need to focus our energy and resolve to make a difference to the things that we can affect, calm down and accept those things that we can't influence and most importantly, know which is which.

A new version for this book
This simple 3-point plan summarises so much of the core concept of Influence that is central to this book.

If we combine the ideas of this book and include them in the serenity prayer, we produce the following lines, which although less eloquent than the original, show the relationship between that prayer and the book's core concepts.

1. Recognise those things we can influence; and do something about them
2. Recognise those things we are actually passive to, and be influential in how we then deal with the fact that we can't do anything about them
3. Distinguish the proper use of the passive from the misuse of it.

When we can do the above our stress will be reduced, our happiness, productivity and success enhanced and our lives will work better.

The Opposite Approach
Engaging with these simple ideas highlights one of the central problems with us as humans, which is: that many of us don't approach the world from this perspective. Instead we spend too much of our time doing exactly the opposite. We try to change things that we have no influence over (like the weather, the boss, the traffic) and not enough time changing the things we actually can change (our mood and our responses to events).

Throwing our energy into trying to change 'problem' situations which are not ours to influence, only makes us more frustrated and stuck.

When we have mistakenly categorised situations or experiences as 'beyond our influence', we naturally miss the opportunities to change the things we can. This in turn causes us to put up with things we don't need to, or to dwell on negative responses that we have failed to notice are within our power to change. This only serves again to make us feel frustrated, stuck and disempowered.

Approaching life from this 'opposite approach', although present in almost epidemic proportions throughout the world, is just not a brilliant or successful recipe for happiness.

Instead I would recommend you keep these three guidelines of the Serenity Prayer in mind, not only whilst working your way through the book, but as a general guide to using these concepts everywhere in your life.

Exercise 5.3
Where can you see that you've been putting too much energy into trying to change something that you can't influence?

(Hint: Think particularly about parents, partners, family members and work colleagues)

Where can you now see that you've not been putting enough energy into changing something that you can influence?

(Hint: Think particularly about those to do lists that never get done, those New Year's resolutions that you keep making, and breaking, each year)

Now you've clearly identified these things, do you think that maybe it's time to do something about them?

Now let's return to the third and final statement:

Statement 3: "I would have been on time but the traffic made me late."

Having worked through the first two statements in much depth, it should already be fairly clear to you that there are big questions to be asked about the factual accuracy of the final statement, and yet how many times is this very statement used everyday?

Again let's assume that they are being factually accurate when they report the traffic was bad, but once again we need to consider the other half of the statement, which is all about how this has caused their lateness.

With this example it might help to explore some of the issues around being late, or being on time, before looking at the example in detail.

Strategy for Lateness
I've spent many intriguing hours working with people who have had a long history of being late. Some of them are relatively happy with their time keeping, as they feel its just part of who they are, but have come to see me because others have a problem with it. Others don't like being late but just find themselves simply unable to get to places on time.

You can probably already start to notice some of the Passive Language being generously sprinkled into the above descriptions of their lateness problems.

One of my approaches with issues such as these is to try and identify exactly what is going on inside the mind of the client, and especially how they see reality, and how that differs from people who are great at timekeeping. Doing this starts to unravel their 'strategy' for being late. This may seem like a strange way to put it, but I would argue that anything that is *that* consistent, must have a sound and dependable mechanism, or internal strategy, that ensures that behaviour is effectively maintained and consistently reproduced. Talking to enough 'late people' has led me to identify the following general issues:

1) Valuation: Being on time is not especially valued as being important:
   a. Punctuality may be seen as a negative attribute - "only uptight people are always on time".
   b. Lateness may be seen as a positive attribute - "it's cool and interesting to be late".

2) Justification: Being a bit late is better than not turning up at all - "at least I turned up, so get over it".

3) Normalisation: "Lots of people are late".

4) Rationalisation: We can't control things like the traffic, so "it's not reasonable to always be able to be on time".

5) Calculation:
    a. Work out what is the **shortest** time it will take to get there, assuming everything goes perfectly smoothly.
    b. Do not factor in time for:
        i.   Unexpected events
        ii. Essentials: Getting ready, finding keys, money, tickets etc.
    c. Assume that this is the time the journey will take.

This leads to some of the classic statements like "The journey to Rachel's house is only 20 minutes. Yet every time I do this journey, something gets in the way, either the traffic is bad or there are road works, and it always takes 40 minutes."

This means they have a small reality conflict. In their world the journey **is** 20 minutes. Yet in reality the journey that **should**, by their estimation or looking at the distance on the map, take only 20 minutes **actually** takes 40 minutes. They need to reassess their stored version of reality 'it takes 20 minutes' with the way things actually are 'it takes 40 minutes'.

6) Preparation: Often in addition to this distorted relationship to time they will also be extra generous with what can be done with the time before leaving.

If they need to leave at 9.20, at 9.15 they will realise they have an extra five minutes to spare before they leave, and instead of leaving early (for some reason that is just not an option!) again they will miscalculate the time something takes, thinking, "Oh that's enough time to have a cup of coffee, feed the dog, check my emails, etc."

Unfortunately once again they are wrong. None of the tasks take the time they allow for it:

They can drink a cup of coffee in five minutes, but not boil the kettle, let it cool down or watch the ten minutes of TV that they like to whilst drinking their coffee.

They can feed the dog in five minutes, but not get the dog into the kitchen, find the new pack of food that someone has put in the wrong place, get the scissors which aren't where they should be, and clean up the dog food that's now got onto their clean clothes.

They can check their emails, but not switch on/restart the computer or the internet, compose an appropriate reply to one or forward one to someone whose email address is not in their contacts folder, where it should be, and instead is somewhere in the inbox.

Looking at this it almost seems as if they plan to be late, but these processes go on unconsciously and automatically and so are 'beneath the radar' of most people's normal awareness. As we have already seen in other sections of this books, such as Negative Wants and Passive Language, if we have no awareness of an issue there is very little we can do about it.

Once the 'strategy for lateness' has been identified, it becomes much simpler to start to make positive changes to issues such as these.

Exercise 5.4
If you are someone with timekeeping issues and you would like to change, then just look through this strategy, which I've summarised briefly below, and start to list the

required changes that need to be made to each and every step.

1) Valuation: What value would you like to put on being on time?
2) Justification: Do you want to continue justifying your lateness?
3) Normalisation: Is everyone late?
4) Rationalisation: Is it really true that you can't control being on time?
5) Calculation: How should you calculate the journey time if you want to be on time?
6) Preparation: How should you prepare?

Here are some further ideas and thoughts to help you resolve these issues:

1) Valuation:
   a. How will you need to see being on time?
   b. How will you need to see being late?

2) Justification: What would it take to lose the justification that it's ok to keep people waiting for you?

3) Normalisation: Being on time is a common trait found in well-respected successful people. Being late is not.

4) Rationalisation: We can't control things like the traffic, so it's logical to plan effectively so that you can be on time.

5) Calculation:
    a. Work out what is the **most likely** time it will take to get there, assuming for a certain amount of problems on the way.
    b. Factor in time for:
        i.   Unexpected events
        ii.   Essentials: Getting ready, finding keys, money, tickets etc.
    c. Assume that this is the time the journey will take and add 10% of extra time on top.

6) Preparation: Stick to your leaving time and be reasonable about what you can **really** fit in before you leave.

It may also be worth considering that there are already times when you are good at time keeping – for almost everyone there are some situations or people that you would not be late for.

Exercise 5.5
Imagine if you had to be at a certain place, for example the Hollywood sign in Los Angeles, by 12pm ten days from now. And if you made it there by that appointed time you would be rewarded with 20 billion US dollars. Those 20 billion US dollars would be yours to use in anyway you chose. You could give it away, spend it on anything you wanted to, do whatever you wanted to do with it - but if you were late you wouldn't get a cent of it - do you think you would make it there on time?

Returning to statement 3: "I would have been on time but the traffic made me late."

Now that we have explored this issue in some depth the standard questions we have been asking about this statement become quite simple to answer.

1. Control: It's become clear that timing is something within our control. There are of course a few exceptions to this, when even the most generous time plan is destroyed by extreme events - but most lateness is due to poor planning rather than unexpected disasters.

2. Power: If the journey normally takes 20 minutes but might take 40 minutes, it is clearly not true that they have absolutely no power over planning to leave at a time that ensures they arrive on time.

3. Nothing they could do: There are a number of things they could to do to be on time, even if the traffic is bad, such as leaving earlier.

4. Options: It is not true that they had no option but to be late.

5. Victim: It's also clear that it wasn't the traffic that really *made* them late. It was a combination of bad traffic and, most importantly, bad planning.

If they can be on time for one thing, because it is important enough, like a plane trip, an important job interview or date, or meeting at the Hollywood sign, even if the traffic is unpredictable, then it follows that their lateness cannot be as linked to 'the traffic' as they have stated. This leaves us with the uncomfortable, but useful, truth that; there was much they could do about their lateness. They, and not just the traffic, were influential in whether they were on time or not.

So we can see in each of these example statements there are a number of things that were not reported entirely accurately.

Once you have a good understanding of the idea of Influence, one of the simplest ways to uncover these inaccuracies is to use the following question:

Key Question A: 'Is that thought, or that statement, accurate and factual?'
When this question is applied, as in the above examples, to the notions of:

1. Control
2. Power
3. Nothing they could do
4. Options
5. Victim

It becomes quite easy to recognise the use of Passive Language.

6. Opinions, Beliefs and Facts

...she knew with absolute certainty she was in trouble. Trapped, and at the mercy of the worryingly dark shape that moved menacingly towards her. The more she twisted and turned the more she realised how completely trapped she was. No good could come of this.

Something about this reminded the piggy of when he had tried to take his new Ikea sofa upstairs. At the turn of the stairs, the sofa became stuck fast and would go no further no matter how hard he pushed and pulled...

Another very useful tool in our search for reality and accuracy is an understanding of the difficulties posed by the presence of opinions, beliefs and facts.

These linguistic tricksters lurk in the shadows of so many conversations. They are much like the biblical tale of Jacob being deceived into marrying the wrong girl because she wore a veil at the wedding to hide her true identity (and to this day, in traditional Jewish weddings, the groom lifts the veil of his bride before the marriage takes place just to check she is his intended partner). Like the veiled bride, opinions (or beliefs) and facts can be equally difficult to distinguish from one another, and the consequences of getting these two different things confused with each other can be just as serious.

Firstly let's clarify what these terms mean.

Opinions and beliefs are really very similar. They are a view or perspective that is held by one person or more; but they are not necessarily facts. That is because they are not based on unbiased evidence; they are based on judgements, guesses or approximations.

Again referring to a dictionary definition helps:

> Opinion: a view, judgement, or appraisal formed in the mind about a particular matter. (*Webster*)

> Belief: a conviction of the truth of some statement. (*Webster*)

Interestingly if we look up what 'conviction' means:

> Conviction: a strong persuasion or belief (*Webster*)

This of course means that a belief is defined as a *belief* about the truth of something.

So beliefs and opinions are judgements that have been made about something, and although:

a) They might be stated with great conviction
b) They might be presented as if they are factual
c) A number of reasonable and intelligent people might agree with those views

it does not follow that those views are always correct or accurate.

Here are some famous examples:

> *"I think there is a world market for maybe five computers."*
> Thomas Watson, chairman of IBM, 1943.

> *"This 'telephone' has too many shortcomings to be seriously considered as a means of communication. The device is inherently of no value to us."*
> Western Union internal memo, 1876.

> *"We think your son Albert might be mentally retarded."*
> Professional opinion given to Albert Einstein's parents.

> *"Who the hell wants to hear actors talk?"*
> H. M. Warner, Warner Brothers, 1927.

> *"We don't like their sound, and guitar music is on the way out."*
> Dick Rowe of Decca Recording Co. rejecting the opportunity to sign up the Beatles, 1962.

> *"Stocks have reached what looks like a permanently high plateau."*
> Irving Fisher, Professor of Economics, Yale University, 1929, just before the Wall Street crash.

Facts on the other hand are just data. They are pieces of information that can be verified independently of the person who presents them. Again referring to a dictionary definition helps:

> Fact: a piece of information presented as having objective reality. (*Webster*)

So the rule we will use in this book to distinguish 'beliefs and opinions' (and from now on, as they are so interlinked, we will treat them as one single thing rather than two different entities) from facts is that:

- Beliefs and opinions are just that - opinions, no matter how strongly they are stated. They depend on someone's judgement of 'truth'
- Whereas facts are accurate accounts of something, independent of the bias of someone's opinion or judgement.[4]

Exercise 6.1
Use this rule to assess whether the following statements are:

a) Beliefs or opinions
b) Facts

For the purposes of this exercise assume that they are either definitely and completely factual or they are not; you have to chose (a) or (b) there is no option (c)!

1.   2 plus 2 is an easy sum, which equals 4.

   (a) Belief/opinion ☐   (b) Fact ☐

---

[4] For those of you with a deeper interest in philosophy, you may reasonably wish to question whether anything is really accurate or true, and who exactly is a completely unbiased independent observer. These are great questions, which we touch on in later chapters but for the purpose of ease of understanding we will use this definition at this point in our journey.

2. Washington D.C. is the current capital city of the U.S.A.

   (a) Belief/opinion ☐   (b) Fact ☐

3. Wolfgang Amadeus Mozart was the most influential Austrian composer of the late 18th century.

   (a) Belief/opinion ☐   (b) Fact ☐

4. Some species of lizards can shed their tails on purpose, for example when escaping a predator, and then re-grow them again.

   (a) Belief/opinion ☐   (b) Fact ☐

5. It is wrong to steal.

   (a) Belief/opinion ☐   (b) Fact ☐

How did you do?

Let's consider the answers one by one.

1)   2 plus 2 is an easy sum, which equals 4.

This, surprisingly, is an opinion.

Most people I ask think it's a fact, because they know that 2+2 does =4, so it must be true. Whilst it's true that 2+2=4, and that *is* a fact as it can be verified independently, it is not a fact that it is an *easy* sum; that part of the statement is an opinion, which makes the whole statement an opinion. Check this out by considering if I asked you to judge these similar statements:

2 plus 2 is everyone's favourite sum which equals 4

2 plus 2 is a hard sum for everyone which equals 4

2 plus 2 can't be worked out by bald people which equals 4

You should have no trouble in recognising them as not true.

Similarly we can also recognise that '2 plus 2 is an easy sum which equals 4' is not true, because a three month old baby does not find this an easy sum. Perhaps if we were to add many more conditions to this statement, for example excluding babies and people who are neurologically incapable of performing simple maths, then it might become a factual statement, but the way it appears in the question, it's just not accurate or true.

2) Washington D.C. is the current capital city of the U.S.A.

This, on the other hand, is a factual statement.

It can be independently verified that the U.S.A has currently designated Washington D.C. to be their capital city.

3) Wolfgang Amadeus Mozart was the most influential Austrian composer of the late 18th century.

This, maybe surprisingly, is an opinion.

Most people are so convinced by the things that are facts (he is documented to have been an Austrian, a composer and alive in the late 18th century), that they ignore the opinion portion of the statement - the idea that he was "the most influential". How do we measure influence, is there an agreed scale we can measure him by to claim he has the highest influence score, which he would need to get to be the most influential? His father was also a composer, and although not *considered* by some to be as great a talent as his son Wolfgang, you could reasonably argue that as he taught his son to play music, he could reasonably be declared the most influential Austrian composer of the late 18th century, simply on the basis that he influenced his son so much.

4) Some species of lizards can shed their tails on purpose, for example when escaping a predator, and then re-grow them again.

This, too, is a factual statement; some lizards can do this.

5) It is wrong to steal.

This is an opinion. You and I may hold this to be true, many people may generally agree that this is true, but there are certainly enough people (professional thieves for example) who don't think this is true. Just because we believe it, and we are in the majority, doesn't make it true.

When people complete this exercise it's quite rare for them to get all the answers right; it just seems that we are not very good at distinguishing our beliefs from facts and the reason for this is we are clever.

That sounds a strange thing to say until you look at why we have beliefs and what they do for us.

The Knowledge Gap
When we find ourselves confronted by a gap in our knowledge about how the world works and what its rules are we begin an enquiry to try and understand what is going on, to fill that knowledge gap.

You can see this in action when watching a child playing with a new toy or using a household object that they are unfamiliar with. There will be much trial and error, pushing, pulling, poking, peering and throwing, trying to work out which part goes where or does what.

Eventually they will come to some decision as to what this thing does, how it works and what it is for. And once they've tested it out and confirmed their findings on a few further occasions this new knowledge about the way this works becomes their blueprint for how similar objects and the world itself works.

This is how we all assess and respond to new or unfamiliar experiences.

This is a very useful approach to the world, as it allows us to apply knowledge acquired in one situation to speed our understanding and competency in another situation. So, the next time we encounter something new, by recognising its similarity to something we've encountered before, we already have a basic idea of what to do to get it to work too.

This approach works even if the new experience isn't at all similar to any previous experience, as it allows us to recognise that this unfamiliar experience is actually similar to other previous times when 'we don't know what this is', and we already have strategy for dealing with those kinds of situations too.

The problem with this is that, because we are so pleased with the good results we've been getting with our new approach, we apply it independently of whether it's the correct or best approach.

China and the Tea Effect
There is a theory that for a few thousand years the future of China was strangled by the brilliant and early invention of the teacup. The theory goes that as the Chinese were fond of tea, they naturally invented an appropriate vessel for drinking it - the teacup, made of china. Thousands of years passed before western cultures came across this extraordinary material and learned the secrets of how to manufacture china for themselves.

However as a result of china being such an amazing and useful material there was no need, it seems, for the Chinese to make much glass, which is rarely found archaeologically in China. When you think about it you probably already know that traditional Chinese houses didn't have glass window panes, they had paper windows, although you might not have known why before.

But there was a greater cost to using china everywhere than simply not being able to see out of your windows, or having no glass based mirrors.

Although the Chinese had been making china since the 6th century Western society didn't have much access to china and didn't start working out how to make it until the 18th century, as a result it developed a mastery of glass instead. From that came the advances in science due to optics including microscopes, telescopes, reading glasses, etc.

In addition to being able to see through it and magnify with it, another important property of glass is that it is chemically very stable. It barely reacts with anything, and so it is great for storing unstable things in and heating things up in. These properties directly led to its usage in the laboratory and in light bulbs and, rather significantly, electrical valves, which were the original components in TV, radios and behind many other modern electrical inventions.

Some experts think that China became so locked into using a particular technology which worked so well in a number of contexts, that they were blinded to the possibilities of another, apparently un-needed substance, glass. With beautiful china but without glass, this episode of China's history is a classic example of how our understanding about the way the world is can affect everything. In this case China was unable to seize the dramatic opportunities available to her western cousins. With the Chinese people's extraordinarily rich history of invention, we can only wonder as to what the world might be like now if they had.

Knowledge Gap and Beliefs

Beliefs are created very similarly to the way a child deals with a new and puzzling object. We discover a knowledge gap where we don't quite understand something but we need to make sense of it. We consider the best possible explanations available; some of them will be inherited from our society, others from interacting with specific influential individuals and some will be as a result of making our own decisions in combination or in spite of the views of others.

Whatever the events were that caused us to adopt those opinions and beliefs, all of them were designed in an attempt to better understand what was really going on. At this level, at least, humans are fundamentally logical. We make decisions about what to believe based on good reasoning and the balance of experience. The problem is that sometimes the information we base our reasoning on, or the small portions of life experience which we use as a guide of how the world works, are not always accurate, and as a result some of the beliefs that people hold as true are not accurate either.

Unfortunately, because we know that we have come to this conclusion rationally and logically, and are certain that we have considered all the evidence, we are convinced that this approximate version of how the world works is an accurate perspective on the world, a truth.

Because we feel we have already examined the evidence enough before we adopted these beliefs it makes it difficult for us as individuals to recognise them as beliefs rather than truth. And if we can't recognise them as needing to be addressed, then we won't address them. This is one of the core reasons why they have so much power and why for so many people they are 'blind spots' and things they find difficult to change.

Once, however we can distinguish these half-truths as beliefs, then changing them and their influence on our world is actually quite easy. After all, who's in charge of our beliefs, if not ourselves?

A valuable tool in distinguishing half-truths and beliefs from facts is to ask:

Key Question B: 'Does everyone think/agree with that?'

Asking this question is an excellent way of testing for accuracy and will help to uncover the presence of beliefs.

For example:

If not everyone agrees that '2 plus 2 is an *easy* sum' then it's very likely to be a belief.

Occasionally with some of the most factual type questions, the 'Does everyone think/agree with that?' question will identify that we are not aware of all the facts.

> *"In Medieval times people thought that the earth was flat and if you sailed too close to the edge of the world you would fall off."*

Does everyone agree with that? You might think they do, but this is one of those inaccurate urban myth 'facts'.

Medieval people apparently were quite certain that the world was globe shaped and not flat. So even if the majority of people agree that something is true, or false, it might be best to check out if all expert opinion shares the same view.

Review the statements of Exercise 6.1 asking the 'Does everyone think/agree with that?' question

1) 2 plus 2 is an easy sum, which equals 4.
2) Washington D.C. is the current capital city of the U.S.A.
3) Wolfgang Amadeus Mozart was the most influential Austrian composer of the late 18th century.
4) Some species of lizards can shed their tails on purpose, for example when escaping a predator, and then re-grow them again.
5) It is wrong to steal.

In this chapter we have begun to recognise how Passive Language, beliefs and inaccuracies so often occur without us even noticing them. Now it's time to look at the consequences and dangers that can arise from not noticing these issues.

7. Consequences of Passive Language

...leaving the sofa in the stairway seemed the only option. For a few days the piggies climbed over or around it each time they went downstairs to the kitchen to make a cauldron of soup, in case a wolf came a calling again, or sighed with annoyance as they climbed upstairs to bed...

In the last two chapters we've looked at the concept of the Passive Perspective and the possible problem that occurs with its use - which is: implying that we can't make a difference to something when, actually, we can. And, as you may recall, I've named this misuse of the Passive Perspective 'Passive Language'. This chapter is designed to get you even more familiar with distinguishing Passive Language by using a new set of tools - The Problem and Suggested Solution Questions.

Importance of Passive Language
But you might reasonably ask yourself, "Is using Passive Language really that much of a problem?"

As you start to use the key questions explained in this chapter it should quickly become clear that, yes, there are massive consequences to using Passive Language.

The Problem Question

The first step is to identify what the statement suggests seems to be the cause of the problem that needs to be addressed. I've called this the Problem Question, as the easiest way to identify it is to ask, "What is causing the problem here?"

The Suggested Solution Question

The next step I've called the Suggested Solution Question. We ask, "What, then, are the solutions to this problem?" Obviously the solutions to the problem will naturally be suggested by the way the cause of the problem has been identified in the first step.

This is a key point, as the way the problem is presented will define what potential solutions are worthy of consideration and which ones don't even register as options. At this point we become blinkered to a whole section of reality, actions and options, which just seem irrelevant to the issue we are dealing with.

I will use Statement two from the earlier chapters to illustrate how these questions can be used to identify Passive Language:
"My boss was really angry and made me upset again today."

Exercise 7.1

Ask and answer the 'Problem Question' in relation to Statement two before reading on; based on the way it is stated what does the statement suggest is causing the problem here?

The Problem Question

In this case the answer to the problem question is that:

- Their boss was extremely angry and caused them to get very upset, and not for the first time.

It appears from the way the statement is made that how upset they feel at work is very dependent on the boss' mood.

Exercise 7.2

Ask and answer the 'Suggested Solution Question', in relation to Statement two, before reading on; what do you think is the solution to this problem, based on the way it's been stated here?

The Suggested Solution Question

Asking the 'Suggested Solution Question' there are really only a few solutions to how upset they are getting at work. The options are:

1. To leave their job
2. To continue working there and continue getting upset
3. For their boss to change

So the options involve big change or no change; changing their job, changing their boss, or continuing to be unhappy and upset at work.

Exercise 7.3

From what you've read, what problems can you see with these solutions?

There are many problems with each of these solutions.

Solution 1 - To leave their job
Although this will get them out of this particular situation it is a fairly extreme solution, as it forces them to leave their job even though they might like other aspects of their work. Additionally it doesn't really address the question of what happens if they come across another difficult person in their next job, and what if that person is a client rather than a boss? Clearly they don't won't to have to leave each job or client meeting every time they come across a 'difficult' person, and yet that is what this solution demands that they do.

Solution 2 - To continue working there and continue getting upset
Again this isn't a great solution in that nothing has changed. The suggestion is that they just live with the fact their boss is unpleasant and they will have a future of getting upset. Once again they are left disempowered by the fact they are unable to influence what happens.

Solution 3 - For their boss to change
This solution has two possible options. The first option, waiting for the boss to leave, has fairly obvious problems, as it is unlikely they can make that happen.

The second option is to actually make the boss change. But unfortunately, no matter how much we may want to, we can't change our boss; it is just one of those things, similarly to the weather in the previous example, that we actually are passive to - we can't really change how other people do things. In fact, most people, the majority of the time, are extremely predictable and rarely change their behaviours. This seems like a strange thing to say in a book about change so let me qualify that.

Why people don't change when they 'really should'

Many people have unhelpful or destructive behaviours that are fairly easy to spot. When you recognise people being this way you would probably hope, and if you have the right kind of relationship with them, might even recommend, that they do something about it. There are three key ways that people avoid change:

1. The problem is that although this need to change may be obvious to almost everyone else; it might not be obvious to the person. If this is the case they will not change.

2. There are other times when the person recognises that their behaviours are not getting them the results they wish for.

    For example:

    They are trying to inspire their staff by pointing out their failures in order to get them to do better. But the staff's performance doesn't seem to improve.

    They wrongly identify the problem as being: the team members need to toughen up and stop being so oversensitive to constructive criticism, and take positive action about their performance issues

    In this case they feel that the other people are the ones needing to change their behaviours. Again in this case they will not change.

3. In other cases they may really wish to change, but if they don't think they can or don't know how to, or are not prepared to do what is required to make those changes, again they will not change.

We have all met people who fit into one of these categories and it's frustrating to watch opportunities for happiness slipping past them, but there is not much you can do, because it's within their power, and no one else's, to influence and change.

Equally, people do make dramatic and radical changes to how they've been behaving for years, but this only happens when **they** decide to. Every therapist will tell you stories of helping people make changes to life long issues, and to later hear how the client's long suffering partner responded to the change by saying, "What's taken you so long to make this change? I've been telling you need to sort this and what to do about it for years". And that's the key. You can't make people change, people can only make themselves change, and to do that they have to be ready to take on that ability to *Influence* themselves and take action.

Returning to our three proposed solutions for dealing with the 'upsetting boss' we can quickly notice that all these are either not very likely to happen (changing the boss) or are about waiting for some external force (such as time passing or the boss moving on or mellowing out) to take action to improve things for the person involved. So based on the way the problem has been stated and solutions that naturally arise from that, the person is completely passive and stuck.

The Escape Option
The other tempting option is for the person to decide that what they need to do is avoid those kinds of troublesome situation. This is the 'escape' option. This produces as much trouble as the other options as; firstly it's almost impossible to avoid situations or people of a certain kind as they can potentially appear at anytime and anywhere.

Secondly bit-by-bit, more and more of the world becomes a dangerous and hostile place, where they can't survive or thrive, and so they have to retreat into an increasingly limited portion of the world where they can feel unthreatened, happy and safe.

Again we can recognise how the passive nature of all these solutions, and the problems these solutions cause, naturally increases their profound sense of disempowerment.

Conclusion

The Problem/Suggested Solution Questions are another useful tool to identify inappropriate usage of the Passive Perspective (Passive Language). We can also see how these types of Passive Statements make it almost impossible for people to find a useful and workable solution to their problems.

At this point life stagnates. And this is really not a good thing at all. Your talents become wasted, your enthusiasm and drive dries up and as we will see in later chapters even your health can suddenly become dangerously at risk.

Keep in mind that if you had just heard someone use the kind of Passive Language that we've been looking at in detail, and you asked them if it was really true:

- That it was their boss who actually made them angry?

They would probably initially answer, 'Yes'.

Although **we** can now see that it's not really reasonable to attribute our state of mind to these external events or people, this is just not how most people would see it. And if this new perspective now seems obvious to you then it's worth remembering the famous French philosopher Voltaire's observation that "common sense is quite rare".

8. Spotting Passive Language

...what was it, thought the piggy, about this elf being tangled in a web, that so reminded him of the stuck sofa?...

It's becoming clear that there is a huge cost to using Passive Language and now you know what it is, you are already more informed about this subject than most people. However, it can still present a major problem as it so often appears in conversation and thoughts as reasonable and factual that we just don't notice it. Becoming aware of when you are using it is, in my experience, absolutely essential to getting a life that you love, and that will take a little practise and a good set of tools.

This chapter introduces some new key tools, and combines them with the ones you have already explored in this book, so that you will be able to recognise Passive Language easily.

Three Tools for Freedom

1. Spotting Key Words
Anytime you use one of the eight words or phrases listed in the following table there is an excellent chance that whatever you said was stated using Passive Language. There are other words and phrases linked to Passive Language, but these are the most common.

Signs
1.   "I feel"
2.   "I have"
3.   "I am"
4.   "It just is"
5.   "They are"
6.   "I can't"
7.   "I get"
8.   "Made me"

In the following chapters we will use this table to help us identify Passive Language.

Sometimes the Passive Language will be hidden, or silent. In the example "I try to be early for appointments, but I have a difficulty with being on time". This statement contains "I have" which is easy to spot, but it also contains a strong sense of "it's just the way I am" although it's not actually said. In some of the examples we will show these silent or hidden Passives in brackets.

See the table below:

Signs	Details
1. "I feel"	
2. "I have"	I have difficulty being on time
3. "I am"	
4. "It just is"	(It is just the way I am)
5. "They are"	
6. "I can't"	
7. "I get"	
8. "Made me"	

There are also some statements, which you should now be able to recognise as obvious examples of Passive

Language as they clearly describe how something took over or took control of them:

- *It just happened to me*
- *The feelings descended on me*
- *He took it away from me*
- *I am helpless*

Please keep in mind that whenever you hear the key words in the table they *suggest* that you have used Passive Language, but it is not always the case, and so using the words is not always problematic.

For example:

"I am a boy."

This phrase contains the key words "I am", and it states something that you are passive too. This is much like the example of "it is cloudy", but being passive to these things is not a problem. It is one of those situations where you simply don't have a choice about it and that's ok.

You will need to use the other tools in the book to help distinguish their appropriate use from their misuse.

2. Mood Spotting
If you are:

- Feeling stuck
- Feeling stressed, frustrated, angry or upset
- Feeling down or guilty
- In a mood
- Moaning
- Complaining

Being unkind to yourself or others
- Losing your sense of humour
- Not heading towards a great life

then the chances are that you are using Passive Language.

The chart below summarises these possible pointers to Passive Language:

Signs
1. "I feel"
2. "I have"
3. "I am"
4. "It just is"
5. "They are"
6. "I can't"
7. "I get"
8. "Made me"
9. Obvious Passives
10. Stuck
11. Moody, Stressed, Unhappy
12. No sense of humour

3. Key Accuracy Questions

The next tool is to ask the key question that we focused on earlier in chapter five:

Key Question A: 'Is that thought or that statement accurate and factual?'

In that chapter we also considered another version of this same question, which helped identify the presence of hidden beliefs:

Key Question B: 'Does everyone think/agree with that?'

Shortcut to Accuracy

There is another additional question that we can ask ourselves to help us distinguish the appropriate from the inappropriate use of the Passive Perspective:

Key Question C: 'Actually, what <u>can</u> I influence here?'

This powerful question will help you to do two things:

1) It will identify if the statement is:

    a. An example of the proper use of the Passive Perspective

    b. An example of Passive Language (which is something to be recognised and then sorted out using the skills later in this book)

If the answer to 'Actually, what <u>can</u> I influence here?' is genuinely 'nothing' as in the example:

Statement: "The weather was cloudy."

Then we have quickly identified this as a good use of the Passive Perspective.

If the answer to 'Actually, what <u>can</u> I influence here?' is genuinely 'something' as in the example:

Statement: "This kind of cold and cloudy weather **gets me down.**"

Question: "Actually, what can I influence here?"

Answer: "Something - my mood."

Then we have quickly identified this as an inappropriate use of the Passive Perspective and therefore an example of Passive Language.

2) It will guide you towards working out what the real problem is and what the solution to it is.

I recommend you use this valuable shortcut question in addition to the other questions that you are now becoming familiar with as you begin to master the skill of recognising Passive Language.

Now you are armed with knowledge that:

- There are three key tools for spotting Passive Language:
    o Spotting key words
    o Mood spotting
    o The key accuracy questions
- Some things are beyond our control
- Some things are within our control
- We are not always completely accurate about how much influence we have in certain circumstances
- When we get these judgements wrong, the consequences are usually limiting to the happiness of our lives

It's time to make a change, by looking at the antidote to Passive Language, Active Language.

9. Active Language

...then he remembered. In a moment of brilliance worthy of his two heroes, the wisest of all pigs, Einstyn and Nils Boar, he had realised that if the sofa can become stuck, then logically if you reverse the pathway that lead to it becoming stuck you can make it unstuck. He shouted to the elf to stop wriggling and to start behaving like his sofa...

Active Language is the very opposite of the stagnating Passive Language, which as we've already seen can have very disastrous effects on your life.

If using Passive Language defines you and keeps you in a position of powerlessness then Active Language is used where you recognise that you do have some influence in a situation. By using Active Language in place of Passive Language it naturally turns it from being a situation in which you seemed powerless and a victim of the events, to being one in which you can do something with this influence and change things for the better.

If Passive Language has a massive negative influence on your future and causes problems in your life, then similarly using Active Language will have a powerful life-enhancing influence on your future.

The Change
So how do we change this restrictive, limiting and life destroying Passive Language into Active Language? The way that I've developed to achieve this is to replace the key passive verb ('have' in the example below):

"I <u>have</u> a fear of dogs."

with a new verb:

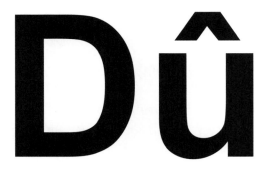

This is a new verb I've had to create, as there wasn't a verb that effectively described the very particular concept that I wanted to express. And as such it needs some introduction.

Dû, Dûing, Dôes, Dône, Dîd
This new verb has a very similar meaning and usage to the verb 'to do', but with some very precise and important limitations.

It is used to describe when someone is unintentionally or unconsciously involved in the creation or maintenance of some feeling, situation, experience or issue.

This is a vital distinction to make as, although it sounds the same as the verb 'to do' when spoken, 'dûing' has no sense of blame attached to it as it is describing something that is generated by your unconscious, unintentionally. The **û** is specifically there to remind us of the **un**conscious and **un**intentional nature of our involvement in this.

So in our example:

"I <u>have</u> a fear of dogs."

This describes the situation in a very passive way. It tells us that the fear is something that just exists and is relatively unchangeable and dependent on the dogs (and maybe your history) and suggests that the fear can only be managed if the dogs stay away.

Converting this into Active Language using the new verb, dû, this becomes:

"I **dû** a fear of dogs."

In this second sentence it's still true you experience fear around dogs, but there is a change in the emphasis as to what is causing the fear. Now we realise that you are involved in the production of the fear (unconsciously and unintentionally), rather than it all being caused by the dog. Following our theme of influence, if you are influential in the process of creating the fear then you will have an influence on its resolution. Suddenly you have become active in the 'fear process', and therefore in finding a solution.

International Dû

As the new word spread across the world, I suddenly found myself in the unfamiliar territory of having to create a word for 'dû' in other languages. This caused a number of issues; one of which was that in some languages, as you've probably already recognised, a word that looks exactly like our dû already exists, although it doesn't have the meaning that has been presented in this book.

The next step then was to decide what word to use in its place; this required lengthy discussions with a number of people from each country involved to try and find a word that was acceptable and expressed the ideas of the dû. This was a very sensitive process as each country's language is very special to its culture and it's people, and any 'foreign' words need to be considered carefully. If you are interested in some of the words that were chosen then please go to the www.duing.org website, which will contain the most up to date list.

Using 'To Dû'

To become more familiar with this new verb and the major consequences it has for us, we will quickly re-examine those three example statements. This time the key passive verbs are underlined in each case.

- "This kind of cold and cloudy weather <u>gets</u> me down."
- "My boss was really angry and <u>made</u> me upset again today."
- "I would have been on time but the traffic <u>made</u> me late."

If we take the first example and use the **dû** word it changes it to:

The weather is cold and cloudy and I **dû** *'getting down'.*

The **dû** has achieved three main things.

Firstly the **dû** has broken up the sentence into two parts. So now we have:

Part one:

"The weather is cold and cloudy"

And, quite separately, part two:

"I **dû** 'getting down'."

Whereas the passive version of the sentence links the two events together (weather and down feelings), the use of the **dû** makes it very clear that actually these two things are not really related to each other and one does not cause the other to happen.

Secondly the **dû** is very jarring, as it's new and just doesn't sound right. Luckily, this strangeness makes us wake up, listen and consider what we have just said. This is why I designed it this way. It helps to increase our awareness of the trouble we were getting into and therefore allows us to start making different choices.

And thirdly, and probably most importantly it makes us recognise that we do in fact have a choice about this (getting down) behaviour. The usage of the **dû** means we are now clearly stating that:

1. The situation has not made the behaviour happen all by itself
2. This is a behaviour that we have 'generated', at some, often unconscious, level.

We know that in its original passive form there were very few options apart from waiting for the weather, time or something interesting to come along and lift our mood. Those are still options in the new active version but we also notice that another key option has now appeared.

- If it's something we are **dûing**
- Then equally, it is something we can **stop** dûing
- And instead **do something else** more life enhancing

Notice in the last line we went back to using the normal English 'do'. This is because the 'something else' you are going to start doing is a conscious decision and is being created on purpose/with intention.

People often get a bit confused with when to use **dû** or **do**. Remember the **dû** is only used when the decision was made/created unconsciously and without intention. Once you have recognised that what you are **dûing** is not getting you what you want out of life, then you make a conscious decision to **do** something else instead.

You may have also noticed that the use of the **dû** word has introduced the idea that the 'feeling down' is behaviour rather than an inbuilt trait, or inbuilt response. Or to put it in its most simple form, the idea that it is:

- Something we **dû**, not something we **have**.

This conceptual shift is also very important, and we will come back to this in Chapter 12 when we will discuss the linguistics behind some of these ideas.

The core effect of the insertion of this simple word '**dû**' is a massive perceptual shift, where:

- We suddenly recognise that the world isn't the way we thought it was

- Just by knowing that we were influential to some extent (although not to blame) in the development of the problem, allows new options to instantly present themselves
- We now know we have a say in choosing how things turn out from now on

The importance of this change cannot be over-emphasised. My experience is that wherever people are stuck in their lives you will find Passive Language and, by the appropriate insertion of '**dû**' change starts to happen naturally.

The ideas of discovering you can influence your life and future has been researched in depth by many authors (Seligman, 1998), (Yapko, 2009). Their observations suggest that there is much to be gained by the power of this perceptual shift alone.

What is new here is an effective strategy for making change. The tools in this book move these ideas from the theoretical to the practical. Once you have recognised when you have taken an inappropriate Passive Perspective and have spotted your Passive Language, change can be rapidly achieved by simply converting those statements to Active Language using the word **dû**.

This usage of **dû** creates a huge shift in our perspective. It is similar to those paradigm shifts mentioned in the introduction, where one set of world views had to be discarded because another new set of information, incompatible with our original views, now made more sense. In this case this use of **dû** creates a personal paradigm shift, as these two perspectives of 'the weather made me down', and 'I am **dûing** down' just cannot be held at the same time, and so one of the perspectives **has** to be discarded.

The question is, which one? Hopefully, having worked through the book, noticing the negative consequences of continuing to hold onto the old inappropriate Passive Perspective, it should help to make the choice easy.

And once you choose to use the word **dû**, change starts to happen. This is due to the nature of the connection between language and the way our thoughts and neurology work. Similar to any other training process, training yourself to change your Passive Language into Active Language actually changes the way your brain cells interact, thanks to a process known as Neuroplasticity.

Neuroplasticity
Neuroplasticity is a slightly complicated name for a very exciting and important way in which the brain learns. In order to make sense of it you first need to have some understanding about how the brain works. To make this as simple as possible I'd first like you to consider two other similar systems, railways and computers.

The Railway System
Imagine a situation where two railway systems have been built independently of each other, one linking town A to town B, and another linking town C to town D. Having separate tracks between these two sets of towns (shown in black in figure 1) makes travelling between towns on different systems, like A and C or D and B, impossible. In order to make the railways more useful and economical it is fairly obvious that if we build two simple branch lines (shown in grey in figure 2) it makes all of the towns accessible whilst using the minimum

amount of track, but still keeping the fast routes between A and B and between C and D.

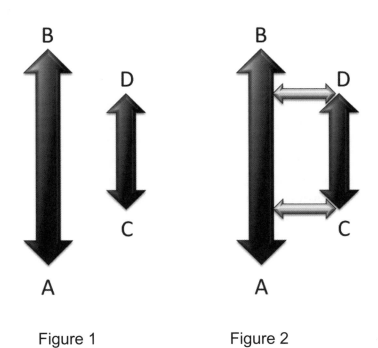

Figure 1   Figure 2

The only complication was making sure that the driver could choose which branch the train took. The solution to this was to create a place where the track could be switched towards C or D (called 'Points' in railway jargon).

The Computer
At a very simplistic level computer circuits work very similarly. Here instead of a train, an electrical current, or signal is directed to various parts of the circuit through wires. Instead of having a set of wires running between each of the points to create separate connections,

branch wires from the main circuits can be used to send the signal anywhere that you wish it to go, with the destination controlled by opening or closing the switches.

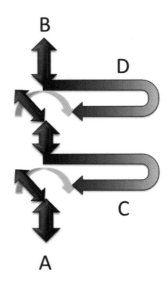

Figure 3. Computer circuits

The Brain
There are some key similarities with the way the brain works and the way the railway and computers systems operate. In the case of the brain, the nerve cells work in a similar way to tracks of the railway system and wires of the computer circuits in the previous examples. However instead of moving trains around, their primary job, like electrical circuits, is to provide a route, or pathway, for the flow of electrical signals/information around the brain. Nerve cells also control the flow of this information, as they have the ability to make connections, technically called synapses, with each other which can be switched

on or off just like the computer circuits switches or the points on the train track.

Certain railway stations are more popular and better connected than others. A station that has trains going to a thousand possible destinations daily, including other well-connected cities, is likely to be more used than one that only goes to one remote village once a week. Some routes will just be more popular and more used than others for a variety of reasons. Similarly in the brain some nerve pathways are more commonly used than others.

However one of the major differences between the rail tracks and computer wiring and brain's pathways is the brain's ability to rapidly (Woolley, Gould, Frankfurt, & McEwen, 1990) change which pathways connect to one another depending on how they are being used.

If a nerve pathway is well used it will become neurologically important. This means, much like a fast track train with fewer stops, it will transmit its signals faster and like a well-used station it will have more connections with other nerve cells. The faster a nerve pathway and the more connections it has with other nerves, the greater an influence it exerts on brain function, and therefore on us, as a whole.

This ability to develop in response to usage is called Neuroplasticity and it works both ways. A pathway that is often used will start to become more influential on the rest of the brain's function, whereas a pathway which is less often used starts to lose it's connections and becomes less important.

As you start to learn something new, such as riding a bike or a new dance, at first there is not much fast and well-connected neurology associated with the new task, and as a result the initial results of learning are usually a bit clumsy. However with some training and time new pathways are formed and the ability to perform the new task becomes easier and more automatic.

Research suggests that the brain stays younger as a result of learning new things (Jankowsky, et al., 2005), and yet we spend so much time doing the same things in the same way.

Exercise 9.1
Pretend that you are picking up a cup of tea. Now physically pretend to stir your imaginary cup of tea. Which direction do you stir first? Clockwise or anti-clockwise? The chances are that you always do it that way.

When you brush your teeth, which area of your mouth do you brush first? The chances are that you always do it that way.

When you butter toast, which way does the first stroke go? The chances are that you always do it that way.

Make your right foot go in a clockwise circle. Keep that going and now using your right hand draw the shape of a 'c' in the air. Did your foot change to anticlockwise?

If the effects of aging on the brain are reduced by learning new things and being stimulated, then is it maybe time for a change?

Using our Brain

When we **dû** 'fear' or 'getting down' we are unintentionally activating parts of our brain which are in charge of creating those feelings. And as we have seen in the previous sections on neuroplasticity, the more we **dû** 'fear', 'getting down' etc., the more we activate and exercise those parts of our brains and the more dominant they become in our lives. Equally if we spend time **doing** (consciously deciding to experience) 'calm' or 'happiness' then we will be activating those parts of our brain which are in charge of those feelings, and the more we activate those, the more powerful a force those brain areas and their attributes will be in our lives.

Therefore once we notice that we are repetitively **dûing** something not very useful, and therefore unintentionally training our brains to learn to be very good at something not very useful, then we can take action. We can stop **dûing** that and instead actively and consciously **do** something more useful with our brains by focusing on the kinds of feelings and behaviours we wish to have more of in our lives. We will cover how to do this in the next chapter.

With that in mind let's move on now to how we apply the core skills of this book:

- Spotting Passives
- Getting clarity
  - ○ Testing them for accuracy
  - ○ Recognising the consequences of staying passive in those situations
- Converting them to Active Language, using '**dû**'

The next chapter enhances your familiarity with these skills by considering a few examples.

10. Application

...as if by magic, the simple advice seemed to work, as she retraced her movements the web fell away from her, and she was free...

Creating lasting change in your neurology and language requires practise. This chapter contains some more examples for you to work through that will help you become skilled in these new ways of thinking.

It may take a little time for this new way of thinking, speaking and approaching life to become familiar and to feel natural. I've found that many people find it a little strange to use 'dû' at first, but as soon as they start applying the skills outlined below and noticing the massive change it brings it all starts to fall into place. And within hours of first getting to grips with it they find themselves automatically starting to use their dû to great effect.

With practise you will be able to take any situation where your life is not working and apply these ideas to start to make things better. The steps are summarised in the diagram that follows.

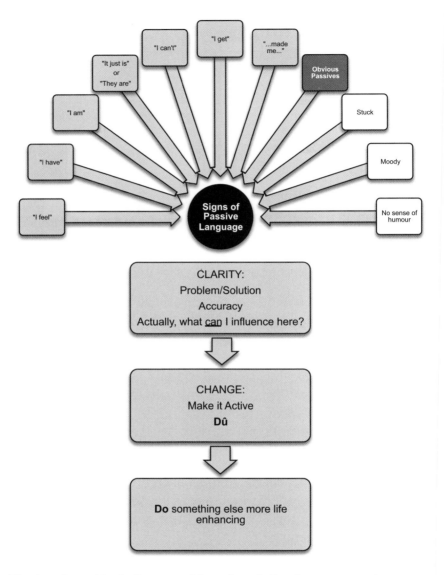

To begin with let's consider the following example, so you can see how this approach works step by step.

Example 1

Imagine someone says:

"I would like to be able to send email messages but computers are so confusing."

Spotting Passives

Let's begin by spotting the passives. A quick check through our list will help.

Passive Checklist

Signs	Details
1. "I feel"	
2. "I have"	
3. "I am"	
4. "It just is"	
5. "They are"	Computers **are** so confusing
6. "I can't"	I would like to (but I can't)
7. "I get"	
8. "Made me"	
9. Obvious Passives	Can't use email functions on the computer
10. Stuck	The sense that *I'm helpless*
11. Moody, Stressed, Unhappy	Not very happy around computers
12. No sense of humour	Absent

From the checklist we can recognise that the Passive Perspective has been used. Referring back to Chapter 7 on the Consequences of Passive Language you may recall we used the 'Problems and Suggested Solutions' and 'Accuracy Question' to become even clearer about whether the Passive Perspective has been used in a reasonable way or has been misused (Passive Language).

Clarity

What is the problem?
From the statement we can see that computers are seemed to be at fault. They are causing 'the problem' by being 'confusing'.

What is the suggested solution?
This naturally suggests that, since the computers are causing the problem, for the problem to be solved the computers need to change, to become less confusing, and then everything will be ok. And until that happens the difficulty will continue to exist and emails will not be a part of this person's life.

Is that accurate? Does everyone think that?
Is it really true that computers are confusing? And does everyone think they are? The answer is clearly, 'no'. This means that computers can't be intrinsically confusing. If some people find then confusing and others find them simple, then it cannot be an absolute fact about their nature, about the way they are. This is an example of a belief being stated as a fact.

Actually, what <u>can</u> I influence here?
If others feel differently about computers then surely it is possible for them to feel differently about computers too?

So to summarise: in the original statement the person has expressed that they would really like to use email, but the reason that it is impossible for this person to achieve this goal is 'nothing to do with them', it's simply because 'computers are confusing'.

But our analysis shows that this perspective isn't very factually accurate; that computers are not either fundamentally confusing or simple to use, it depends on who is using them and how they feel about them.

Recognising the consequences of staying passive in those situations

Now of course this particular situation isn't the worst thing that could happen in someone's life, although being able to access email has become a fairly major part of most people's daily existence. Certainly, at the least, it will cause a degree of frustration, it might also make them feel a bit incompetent and out of touch with today's reality. But the bigger problem is that whenever these kinds of limiting perspectives appear, they stop the person from being able to do whatever they want in the world, and so they start to learn that there are certain 'no go' areas in their life. The more of these there are, the more they expect to find them in other situations and gradually bit by bit their access to the world gets shut down, not because they couldn't thrive in those new arenas but because they think they can't.

So based on all the above, it is fairly obvious that this is an example of Passive Language, which mean's it's time to convert the passive into the active.

Converting it into Active Language, using dû

"I would like to be able to send email messages but computers <u>are</u> so confusing."

We have identified that the passive word is 'are', so the sentence gets converted to:

"I would like to be able to send email messages."

and

"I **dû** confusion about computers."

This, as I have mentioned before, is a very important moment. It has two main effects.

Firstly, and most significantly, it creates a perceptual change in which you suddenly see the whole situation completely differently. Instead of it being classed as something that you were the victim of, you now fully take the role of being influential (but not to blame) in the issue. Discovering that you are the major, yet unconscious, player in the creation and maintenance of this issue has a massive and immediate impact. The instant you see it in this new and more accurate way you realise that you are the powerful force that can choose to continue maintaining this problem in your life, or to decide that it is not going to be this way any more. Maybe, rather surprisingly, there is not much else that you need to do; as this apparently small shift is so significant in the way we suddenly see things. It appears that once you have chosen to simply no longer have that poor relationship to computers, then, as you are in charge of that relationship, it will change.

The second major effect of using **dû** is that it suddenly offers up a new set of practical solutions. The process of using the opportunity the dû provides can best explained as a set of simple steps:

1. Recognise what you are **dûing**

    In this case you are **dûing** confusion about computers. Recognising this will naturally have the effect as described above of bringing back your sense of power and influence in this situation.

2. Work out how would you like to feel about this instead

Now that you are no longer stuck with **dûing** 'confusion' you are free to choose how you feel about 'computers'. So how would you like to feel about them? The answer to this question is usually the opposite of how you currently feel (or are **dûing**) about them.

In this case the opposite of 'confusion' is something like 'clarity' or 'confidence'.

3. Use your brain to build the good feelings.

As we have seen in the section on neuroplasticity **dûing** confusion activates those parts of the brain that have the ability to make things seem more complicated than they actually are. Conversely, activating those opposite parts of the brain that can think clearly and calmly allows us to **do** clarity.

So all you then have to do is simply start **doing** clarity, on purpose, instead of unintentionally **dûing** confusion.

Let's now work through some of other examples:

"My boss was really angry and made me upset again today."

Spotting Passives
Again we need to start by spotting the passives. Use the checklist below as before.

Passive Checklist

Signs	Details
1. "I feel"	
2. "I have"	
3. "I am"	
4. "It just is"	
5. "They are"	
6. "I can't"	
7. "I get"	
8. "Made me"	He made me upset
9. Obvious Passives	My happiness depends on the boss' mood
10. Stuck	I keep getting upset at work
11. Moody, Stressed, Unhappy	Stressed
12. No sense of humour	Absent

Based on this checklist this is clearly showing up as using the Passive Perspective.

Clarity

Again using the 'Problems and Suggested Solutions' and 'Accuracy Question' we can become even clearer about whether the Passive Perspective has been used in a reasonable way or has been misused (Passive Language).

As we've already covered this phrase in some detail in previous chapters (remember the idea about the boss not being able to be a puppeteer), we can quickly recognise that is an example of Passive Language

Actually what <u>can</u> I influence here?

As we've already discussed, you can't really change your boss. Clearly the person you have the biggest influence over is you and, in this situation, the thing you have the most influence over is your upset.

So, once again we can confirm that this is an example of Passive Language, which means it's time to convert the passive into the active.

Converting it into Active Language, using dû

Having identified the passive key words 'made me' we can split the sentence into two and add **dû**. The sentence then becomes:

"My boss was really angry."

 and

"I **dîd** upset again today."

I would expect that the phrase "I **dîd** upset again today" sounds really odd.

Have you ever heard someone say it before? Probably not - as it's simply not the way people talk. However, if people did talk using the Active Language patterns presented in this book an interesting thing would happen.

If the person had understood enough of this book to have:

- Recognised the Passive Language
- Changed it into Active Language
- Gained this new more accurate perspective of what is actually going on
- Recognised that they are influential in the solution to the issue

Then at that point they will have recognised that it's just not reasonable to have this new perspective and insight on the reality of what's going on and still cling to that old point of view that the boss caused the upset and there is 'nothing they can do to change it'.

Their personal usage of the word **dû** suddenly makes it clear to them that they need to be in charge of the resolution of this issue; which is really quite simple. All they need to do is to no longer **dû** upset about the boss and choose to **do** something more useful. This involves the same ideas as explained in the section on clarity around computers, discovering how you would like to feel in that situation (probably calmness and acceptance) and then activating those parts of the brain that are in charge of those feeling instead.

So, if you are someone who keeps finding themselves upset, maybe it's time to not **dû** that upset anymore?

Using this book on others - avoid this!
It's probably worth noting at this point that I strongly recommend that the purpose of this book is to change your language and perspective for the better and through that change your neurological function too. However I would strongly warn you against using it on others, as that is not the purpose or design of this idea.

Philosophically I believe the world would be a much better, happier and nicer place if more people took on the idea of personal influence and moved away from having to find something or someone to blame when things aren't going so well. However, I equally don't believe that it is my place or yours to start giving uninvited feedback to people on the way they are using Passive Language. Firstly it wouldn't be helpful without a long explanation as to why these things are important and what is meant by passive and active, and secondly without the detailed explanation, and especially in depth reference to the ideas of influencing, **dû** and blame, it would just appear that you were being rude and offensive.

You will have to excuse me as I will repeat this warning and the section about blame and responsibility in a number of sections throughout this book. The reason for this is that there will be some readers who, like me, tend to skip sections of a book as they feel they aren't relevant to them or want to get to the most important sections, but these points are just too important to miss out on.

Now we will explore another in the same way.

"I would have been on time but the traffic made me late."

Spotting Passives
Again we need to start by spotting the passives. Use the checklist below as before.

Passive Checklist

Signs	Details
1. "I feel"	
2. "I have"	
3. "I am"	
4. "It just is"	
5. "They are"	
6. "I can't"	
7. "I get"	
8. "Made me"	The traffic made me late
9. Obvious Passives	My being on time depends on something I can't control
10. Stuck	I'm a victim of the traffic

11. Moody, Stressed, Unhappy	The traffic ruined my mood
12. No sense of humour	Absent

Clarity

Once again, from our consideration of this in the earlier chapters using the ideas of 'Problem and Suggested Solution' and 'Accuracy Question' (was the traffic solely responsible for your lateness) this shows up as using the Passive Perspective.

Actually, what <u>can</u> I influence here?

You can't change the traffic, but you can, of course, change your arrival time by increasing the length of time you allow for your journey.

So finally it's time to do something about this.

Converting it into Active Language, using the word dû

Having recognised the passive phrase 'made me' we can split the sentence into two and add **dû.** The sentence then becomes:

"The traffic was really congested."

 and

"I **dîd** late."

or

"I **dîd** not allowing enough time for the journey."

or

"I **dîd** poor planning."

Of course one of the problems with using this active approach for the person who is late is they no longer have a very good excuse for why they were late. Interestingly most people were never very fooled before by the overused 'traffic excuse', as deep down we all already know there's only a very few occasions when there is good and unavoidable reason for being late anyway.

Notice again that the phrase "I **dîd** late" or any of the other variants above still sounds really odd. Remember that is part of the design of this approach, to wake up your brain from just putting up with the sort of half-life that naturally comes from speaking and thinking in Passive Language.

In time the sound of it will become a bit more usual for anyone adopting this way of thinking, but even when it's become more familiar it will still have the power to make you stop and remember that it's time for you to take action and influence the situation for the better.

Exercise 10.1
What follows are some common examples of Passive Language Patterns for you to apply this approach to. Run through the steps we used in each of the examples. Use the:

- Checklist - to work out what are the words that makes them Passive Language Patterns
- Clarity - use the 'Problem and Suggested Solution' and 'Accuracy and Influence Questions' - to confirm the Passive Language Pattern
- Turn the passive into an active - using the word **dû, dûing, dîd, etc.**

1. "I feel angry about the way my parents treat me."
2. "I try not to be late, but I have difficulty with being on time."
3. "I am bad with new people."
4. "It's always been the same, I am shy. It just is the way I am."
5. "I am just one of those people who can't understand maths."
6. "I get stressed."
7. "What she said made me feel fat."

I provided some of the possible ways of working through these examples in final section in the book called 'Answers' but I'd recommend working through them one at a time and pausing between each example to check your solution with the one I have provided, so you can identify how well you've mastered these skills.

11. Misunderstanding and Controversy

...although she was now free, the dark shape that crouched near the web moved towards her...

Now that we've covered the core themes and arguments for this approach, hopefully you will have seen the potential of:

- Recognising these hidden language patterns
- Recognising the issues that are maintained by remaining passive to something that actually we can powerfully and positively influence
- Transforming your language to Active Language by using **dû**

so you can minimise the upset and stuckness in your life and use your energy to be engaged in more interesting and life enhancing pursuits.

These concepts can be like dynamite in making astonishing changes in your life. But like dynamite, they have a few potential issues attached to them. One, as I have already mentioned, is that once you have noticed the possibilities of how this perspective makes your life much simpler, better and less stressful, you may be tempted to teach other people the 'error of their ways'. This usually involves offering very well meant advice to them as to where they are going wrong and what they need to do to change things for the better. Please do not do that. Although you might be right, and your advice may be exactly what they need to hear, there are few things more irritating than someone giving advice, giving us 'feedback', or pointing out our mistakes when we haven't asked for it. The most likely outcome of such 'helpfulness' is for them to ignore your advice and get very offended - and if you tell them they are '**dûing**' offended it will probably not make it any better! So please, no matter how tempting it is, don't intervene directly in their lives in this way. These concepts are quite tricky to take on even if you are ready to hear them, and if you are not ready to hear them, almost impossible to 'get'. They will be more likely to give these ideas a chance if they come to them in their own time; you can certainly discuss the concepts with them, and direct them, if they are interested, to resources, such as this book or any of the related seminars, but be very wary of intervening any more than that, unless they have given you express permission to do so.

Linked to the ideas above is the second issue, that of 'misunderstanding'. These concepts have to be approached very delicately and patiently as they have such a possibility of being dismissed out of hand for their sheer contentiousness. Whenever I am asked about my work by journalists, they always want a small bite size version that summarises what I do. This seems very reasonable, yet with ideas as large and open to misinterpretation as these it's a very difficult thing to deliver.

If you consider the passive sentence "When he shouted, I got upset", then without the detailed exploration that you've engaged with throughout this book, it's very easy to misunderstand the true meaning of our Active Language sentence. When they hear "he shouted and then you '**dîd**' upset", then unless they know how **dîd** is different from **did,** they might, quite reasonably, think that we were being quite thoughtless, compassionless and uncaring. As you now know being accused of this would be quite ironic, as it is the unintentional use of Passive Language, and the limitations that comes with it, that keeps people stuck. Any approach that involves leaving these kinds of limitations intact, however well meant or caring isn't really going to help that person in the long run. However it still remains true that unless the person has asked you directly for some help, it's just not appropriate to start wading in with active revisions of what they have said, as it will only sound like you are saying they are to blame for what happened.

The third issue that can arise concerns Influence, which is a core concept in itself throughout this book; this can also be an obstacle for many people for two reasons. One reason, as mentioned in the sections on Influence and **dû**, is that some people confuse these ideas with being blamed for something (as in the example above). The second reason is that then your future is in your hands, as Erica Jong says:

> Take your life in your own hands, and what happens? A terrible thing: no one to blame.

And for many of us that doesn't sound too good; the idea of having to be in charge of all the decisions in our lives and the consequences of those choices can seem overwhelming and having someone else to blame can often seem an easier option.

I hope with the step-by-step, detailed explorations of the subject so far that you will have avoided most of the traps above. If so this will allow us to venture further into even more unfamiliar territory.

Up until now we have applied these concepts to general daily life, noticing how liberating and life changing this could be in both your future and other people's. What follows now is a fairly natural progression of the application of these concepts, but to a field where at first you might not think they really have any place or relevance; the field of health.

12. Limiting and Labeling people

..."I am so sorry", exclaimed the embarrassed laundry spider. "I really should have taken my washing line down last night, but friends came round with some whiskey and cards and we, well we played poker all night and I fell asleep. I am so sorry. If there is anything I can do to make amends, please do let me know."...

In this chapter we are going to explore some deeper issues that occur with the use of Passive Language, and to begin with we will look at its potential to profoundly impact people's health.

In 1972 psychologist Dr. David Rosenhan started an interesting experiment (Rosenhan, 1973), and although 1972 is now some time ago the experiment and its findings are still enormously important and valid today.

Rosenhan asked eight of his friends, three psychologists, one graduate student, a paediatrician, a psychiatrist, a painter and a housewife, if they would help him. Following instructions to neither wash or shave for a few days they were to present themselves to their local hospital complaining of a single symptom, that they were hearing voices in their heads, and the voice was saying 'thud'. He chose the word 'thud' as he had never come across a case of anyone hearing voices with such obviously cartoonish problems in any psychology literature. They were asked to feign no other symptoms and to answer truthfully all other questions about themselves.

On presenting their symptoms to the emergency room's medical staff each one of the pretend, or pseudo, patients was immediately admitted to a psychiatric ward. They had successfully achieved the first goal of the experiment, to be considered psychologically unwell enough to be admitted to hospital purely by presenting a made up symptom.

Following their admission to the psychiatric ward they were then to move into the second phase of the experiment and, following the instructions that Rosenhan had given them at the start of experiment, they told the medical staff that the voice had now gone and they felt fine and would like to be discharged and go home. They were also instructed to gain their release simply by adopting normal behaviours. The shortest time it took for release was 7 days, the longest 52 days. None of the pseudo patients were detected as feigning illness and all but one were admitted with a diagnosis of schizophrenia and were eventually discharged with a diagnosis of 'schizophrenia in remission', meaning they still had a mental illness, it just wasn't currently causing them any problems.

In many cases their normal behaviour after being admitted was seen as more evidence of their illness; on observing one of the pseudo patients writing notes (to be used in the write up for the experiment) a nurse noted "engages in writing behaviours".

Rosenhan published his unsettling findings in the prestigious journal 'Science'. The main message he wanted to get across was that it's not difficult to be misdiagnosed as being mentally ill, but it is very difficult to get rid of that diagnosis, and the meanings that has about you, once it's been made. He suggested that psychiatric labels tend to have a longevity that physical medical labels do not and once the label has been given, everything a patient does is interpreted in accordance with that label.

Rosenhan concluded his paper by stating that he didn't pretend to have the solutions to these issues but was encouraged by certain approaches that showed promise one of which was:

> "...facilities...that...tend to avoid psychiatric labels, (and) to focus on specific problems and behaviors..."

What Rosenhan insightfully points out in his paper is how 'labelling' can have a very negative impact on how that person's case is viewed therapeutically, how that label might adversely affect their future and that maybe we need to consider whether labels/diagnosis are always used in a useful way.

Purpose of Labels
So why do we label people with an illness?

It seems fairly obvious that most people find it very helpful to be given a clear diagnosis. Knowing what we are dealing with helps many of us make some decisions as to what we need to do to get well again. This will usually result in some labelling. "I have arthritis", "I am bi-polar", "I have depression", "I am a depressive", etc. This is not always bad, but as we can see from Rosenhan's experiment this is not always good either, as labels tend to stick to us for sometime. Having read this book up to this point you should notice some words in the above phrases that alert us to the possibility of Passive Language.

The Stickiness of Labels

Labels are sticky, and although Rosenhan points out labels about mental health issues seem to last longer than physical ones, the physical ones can also hang around for a very long time too. But why do they stick? A quick bit of simple grammar is useful here to explain some terms we will be using to explore why this is.

Consider the phrase:

"He is kissing the girl."

This sentence contains amongst other things a verb and a noun:

The verb - the action word of the sentence, what is he doing in the sentence - he is kissing. So the verb is 'kissing'.

The noun - the thing he is kissing - so the noun is 'the girl'.

Exercise 12.1

Underline the nouns in the following phrases.

"I have arthritis."

"I have two feet."

"I am bi-polar."

"I have a car."

"I have depression."

"I have brown hair."

"I am a depressive."

The answers are on the next page.

If you have followed the simple grammar lesson you should have underlined the words in the phrases as below:

"I have <u>arthritis</u>."

"I have two <u>feet</u>."

"I am <u>bi-polar</u>."

"I have a <u>car</u>."

"I have <u>depression</u>."

" I have brown <u>hair</u>."

"I am a <u>depressive</u>."

However unfortunately there are some words that appear in these sentences looking like they are nouns (the things, objects, people, places), but are actually verbs (action words) that have got confused with nouns. These are technically called Nominalisations.

Nominalisations and Nouns
So are those underlined words true nouns or nominalisations? And is it that important?

First we need to work out how to tell a noun from a nominalisation. The easiest way to do this is called the 'wheelbarrow test' which is first mentioned by two very inventive researchers and therapists, Grinder and Bandler (Grinder & Bandler, 1975). They suggest, that if you find a noun you ask, "Can I put it in a wheelbarrow?" If we can put it into a wheelbarrow (and the wheelbarrow can be a big as you want it to be, so if needed we could even fit a planet in it) then it is a noun, if not it's a nominalisation.

Looking again at the phrases above we can quickly spot that the following underlined words:

"I have <u>arthritis</u>."

"I am <u>bi-polar</u>."

"I have <u>depression</u>."

"I am a <u>depressive</u>."

which seemed like nouns, are actually nominalisations, and this is extremely important.

Stuck Nouns and Life Changing Verbs

There is a fundamental difference between nouns and verbs, and that is nouns are by their nature fairly static things that have an existence. By that I mean they exist whether you are engaging with them or not.

"He is kissing the girl."

In this phrase 'the girl' is a noun as she can fit in a wheelbarrow and still exists whether he is kissing her or not.

Nominalisations on the other hand do not exist as static things, because they are actually verbs, which are words that represent actions or processes, not things.

"I saw his dance yesterday."

"He gave me a kiss."

In this phrase the 'dance' and the 'kiss' are nominalisations, because, you can't put them in a wheelbarrow, and as soon as the dance or the kiss stops, it no longer exists.

As soon as we notice the presence of a nominalisation we can recognise that something that is actually an action, a process, something that is changeable and active has been transformed, by language, into a noun. Unfortunately, when it is transformed into a noun it misleads us into thinking that it has all the qualities, like being static or relatively unchangeable, that nouns, or 'things', have.

In the examples:

"I have arthritis."

"I am bi-polar."

"I have depression."

"I am a depressive."

the use of these nominalisations, which makes them appear like nouns, gives these conditions a static-ness that is disempowering and in fact obscures something very important about their nature, that they are in a constant process of flow and change.

Nouns and Verbs in Medicine
With the small understanding of medical science that follows we can start to see that instead of describing these illnesses/conditions (note that these terms too are also nominalisations) as 'static' nouns, it is much more reasonable to convert them back into verbs and describe them as processes.

When medical science looks at disease and illness it sees the illness as consisting of a set of 'disease processes' and 'body responses'. In the section that follows I've used the **bold** formatting to identify the verb/action/process/response words.

If we look at the medical understanding of getting **infected** by bacteria we can see that medical textbooks describe a **series of actions** that the body takes to try and **remove** and **recover** from the presence of the **invading** bacteria. This **process** of **engaging** in battle with the bacteria involves the **construction** and **release** of many hormones and other bio-chemicals, the **movement** and **activation** of cells and proteins, each dynamic wave that the defence mechanism **throws** at the invader is individually **tailored** to find the best way to **respond** to the threat. Some attempts to **overpower** the bacteria are better than others and the symptoms will **come and go** depending on what stage the recovery is in, hopefully with the invader finally being **overcome** and with the body being able to '**scale down**' it's defence processes and **bringing** itself back to normal function.

In this brief description of the infection process and elements of the inflammatory response we can see how much action and process is involved in repelling the invader. Shorthand for this is to say, "I had an infection", which is obviously much easier to say than all of the above; but this shorthand no longer conveys the process nature of the experience. It's become a noun, a nominalisation.

When people say, "I have a chronic (long standing) infection", the words convey a sense of how this isn't a process, it's a thing. However, a chronic infection could be more accurately be seen as the above processes not yet having worked to completion, and this contains a different sense; a sense that work is still on-going in recovery rather than recovery having stopped.

If we look at arthritis, which literally means inflammation (-itis) of a joint (-arthro), we can see that the body is engaged in the process of creating an inflammatory response, relatively similar in many ways to the response to the bacteria above. Again once when it's seen as a process it loses that sense of stuckness and illness and starts to become something that has much more potential for change.

Consider the two descriptions of the same illness/events:

1. Arthritis
2. Your body being involved in an inflammatory process (which is fundamentally designed to mend and heal you) concerning your joints

The first description makes it sound like it is something you just have.

The second description contains the idea that it is a process, and it immediately brings with it a sense that there is much more chance of change, and as a theme of this book, maybe something you could have an influence over, to some degree or other.

If we take these ideas to their natural conclusion we see a linkage to the core concepts of this book. In describing the illness as a noun rather than a series of events or processes we remove the sense of being active in the illness/recovery process and encourage the sense of being passive in our relationship to the illness. Converting it back into Active Language, which is much more in line with medical understanding of the process behind the illness, gives us back some influence as to the way our body can respond to the illness.

In the next chapters we will combine these ideas of the activity of biological processes that are cornerstones of such 'high church' scientific pursuits as pathology (the study of disease processes), immunology (the study of the immune system activity) and histology (the study of cells) with this book's language skills. This will allow us to consider what might be gained by applying these concepts in practical terms to our lives. These grammatical ideas are not yet naturally a part of medical student education, but it's interesting to wonder what would happen if they were?

13. Healthy Happy Brains

...the piggy and the elf were taken aback to find how delightful and well mannered their new friend the laundry owner was. It seemed he had had a life where he was determined to have seized every opportunity that came his way and to relish all life had to offer. And any fear they had had completely vanished as he began to tell extraordinary tales of the people he had met and the sights he had seen whilst on tour with the rock band 'The Spiders from Mars'...

So far we have discovered the idea that medicine fundamentally sees health and disease as dynamically active processes. But how can we utilise this important scientific perspective in enhancing our own health?

This chapter looks at a set of very important illnesses that account for a massive amount of GPs' consultation times. Amazingly, the prevalence of anxiety and depressive disorders in patients who frequently attend general practice is between 40% and 60% (Neal, Heywood, Morley, & al., 1998) (Baez, Aiarzaguena,

Grandes, Pedrodo, Aranguren, & Retolaza, 1998) (McFarland, Freeborn, Mullooly, & Pope, 1985), and in the National Office of Statistics report of 2000 (Singleton N., 2000) over 16% of adults reported having a 'neurotic disorder' (panic attacks, obsessive compulsive disorder, anxiety, depression, phobia). As a result these issues affect the health and wealth of the nation and society, almost as much as that of the individual.

An Active Approach

If you want to gain something from this discussion of a new perspective on mental health issues, it is essential to have read and understood the sections on influence and blame - otherwise what follows will be very difficult to put into any kind of useful perspective.

Depression

If you have ever had the misfortune to suffer from (or more precisely **dû**) depression you may have noticed a certain set of ways of thinking and interpreting the world seemed to sneak into your mind during your depression that coloured how you felt about everything. Many other authors (Yapko, 2009), (Bolstad, 2002), (Seligman, 1998) have written about this tendency to unconsciously alter our experience, so I will not go into immense depth about the style of thinking involved. Suffice to say; somehow when we 'get' depressed we seem to suddenly be rather good at having a tendency to focus on all the bad things in our life. We find it easy to exclude all information that may lead to happy feelings and develop an unfailing instinct to be able to interpret anything that may be seen as positive as somehow bad, flawed or not that good in the long run. This is all topped off with a sense of inability to make any difference to those bleak feelings or our future, which in turn creates a profound sense of disempowerment and hopelessness.

Recognition of these tendencies is pivotal to understanding and changing the nightmare of depression and as such is incredibly important, but of even greater significance is the recognition that we are actively thinking something and that it is those kinds of thinking patterns that are actually the 'depression'. This, as Rosenhan suggested in the last chapter, is the idea of moving away from labelling it as an illness, and instead to start considering it as a set of behaviours.

As soon as we do that we move from **having** an illness, which is something we just have to live with, suffer, wait to lift, struggle with, fight or overcome, to the possibility that it is an active set of processes, something that, unconsciously and without properly choosing, we are **dûing**, and therefore something we could not **dû**.

This of course brings us full circle back to the core idea of the book, passive and active, having or **dûing**.

If we take a core statement of depression:

"I am depressed."

and apply our toolkit from Chapter 8:

Passive Checklist

Signs	Details
1. "I feel"	
2. "I have"	
3. "I am"	I am
4. "It just is"	(It is just the way I am)
5. "They are"	
6. "I can't"	

7. "I get"	
8. "Made me"	
9. Obvious Passives	Yes
10. Stuck	
11. Moody, Stressed, Unhappy	Unhappy
12. No sense of humour	Absent

Based on this checklist this is clearly showing up as using the Passive Perspective.

Clarity

Again using the 'Problems and Suggested Solutions' and 'Accuracy Question' we can become even clearer about whether the Passive Perspective has been used in a reasonable way or has been misused (Passive Language).

We can see that the way the phrase has been set up puts us in a very passive position as our main option is having to deal with **it** in someway (fight, cope with it, wait for it to go, etc.) However if we look at the word depression we can see that although it looks like a noun it can't be put in a wheelbarrow, and so it is actually a nominalisation. This means that although depression isn't actually an 'it' or a 'thing', the Problem Question suggests that 'it' is the problem.

As discussed in the last chapter there are some big problems that occur as a result of thinking something is a 'thing' when it's not.

Imagine if someone decided that the cause of all the world's problems was something called 'x'. They might then decide to fight it, to gather it all up, lock it away and destroy all of it. This might work, you could collect it all and destroy it if 'x' were guns, or explosives. It would take a long time but it might be possible.

Imagine if 'x' were dance, songs, or thoughts about money, or about terrorism. Could you collect those 'things' and destroy them? The answer to both questions is obviously 'no'. Because guns are a noun, a thing, but dance, songs, or thoughts about money or terrorism, and depression, are not nouns, they are nominalisations/verbs.

Unfortunately in this example the Problem has been identified as that 'thing', 'depression'. This means that the 'Suggested Solution' naturally therefore suggests that we should do something like 'fight it', but this isn't going to be very effective, as we now know that that the thing we are trying to fight doesn't actually exist as a 'thing', because it is a nominalisation/verb.

Actually what <u>can</u> I influence here?
Following our discussion about Influence, clearly the person you have the biggest influence over is you and, in this situation, the thing you need to have the most influence over is the way you are currently experiencing (and, we could say, choosing, albeit unconsciously, to see) the world.

So, once again we can confirm that this is an example of Passive Language, which means it's time to convert the passive into the active.

Converting it into Active Language, using dû
By inserting **dû,** the sentence becomes:

"I am **dûing** depression."

Remember it's ok if this phrase sounds very strange, I designed it this way to help you recognise the Passive Language. Imagine if you are the person with depression and you hear yourself saying "I am depressed" and change it to "I am **dûing** depression", then, using the concept of Influence covered previously, how does saying it in that way suddenly make you feel different?

Having created programmes that have worked with thousands of people suffering with depression, this change of perspective from passive to active has revolutionised their future. It's not the whole story, as there are some more steps they need to take to work out how to do something differently, but that moment of recognition of their personal power in a situation in which they thought they were powerless was the pivotal point of change for them.

One client summed up that moment of change:

"The last session was incredible - everything has been going well since.

The fact that one can move oneself out of hideous 'depression' in one hour is pretty incontrovertible evidence that it is optional...

Something really sunk in, and I feel like I'm learning more and more..."

Some of you reading this might have been led to believe in a more biological model of depression; one of the commonest of these is the idea that there are not enough of certain neurotransmitters in your brain to feel happy, and therefore a prescription is the appropriate solution for these issues. This seems very reasonable and is a very commonly held belief amongst people whose main approach to healthcare is to use prescriptive drugs. However it might surprise you to discover that this is not a universally accepted or well-documented model. One paper that raises huge questions about this perspective was published by a team led by Professor Kirsch, who studied all the other studies about the effectiveness of modern antidepressants. The studies focused on the new generation of antidepressants, the 'selective serotonin reuptake inhibitors' (SSRIs). SSRIs are the newest antidepressants and include fluoxetine, venlafaxine, nefazodone, and paroxetine and are hypothesized to normalize the brain chemicals that affect mood. He reports "antidepressant medications have reported only modest benefits over placebo treatment, and when unpublished trial data are included, the benefit falls below accepted criteria for clinical significance." (Kirsch, Deacon, Huedo-Medina, Scoboria, Moore, & Johnson, 2008)

What Professor Kirsch is saying is that those antidepressant medications achieve no more change than the usage of pills that contain absolutely no medication (placebos). This raises serious questions about the concept that the neurotransmitters are really the key problem in depression. In addition it raises some interesting questions about the effectiveness of placebos, which we will consider in the next chapter.

Even if we subscribe to the 'problems with neurotransmitters' model, we should still recognise that production and release of neurotransmitters are part of an active process. Neurotransmitters are the chemicals that allow the signal from one nerve to cross the tiny gap to the next nerve at the junction (technically called a synapse) where the nerves meet. A number of processes need to occur for the signal to be transmitted across this gap:

1. Enough of a signal needs to be produced in the first nerve to stimulate adequate production of the neurotransmitters for the possibility of the signal being transmitted to the next one.
2. Enough of the correct factors need to be in place for the neurotransmitters to be produced to carry the nerve signal across the gap between the nerves. These include just how recently the nerve has transmitted a previous signal, how excited the person is, what time of day it is, what phase of the menstrual cycle it is, etc.
3. This effective nerve signal transmission depends on a kind of tug of war between different nerve groups. Some nerves in the area are specifically designed to prevent the nerve signal transmission. They act like a brake, stopping the overuse of that nerve junction. Other groups of nerves work to help pass the signal across the synapse. For the signal to continue across the synapse the 'helper' nerves will need to be more active and strong than the other set of 'preventer' nerves.

Even looking at just three of the multitude of factors which affect transmission we can see there are many active processes going on, so the problem is not really with the *neurotransmitters*, it's with the *process of neurotransmission*.

Instead of "I have bad neurotransmitters" what if we move towards (again with a good understanding of the ideas of Influence) the statement "I **dû** poor neurotransmission."

This active understanding of the process has much more opportunity for change than the static idea that is suggested by the Passive Statement.

Once again, as long as we have avoided the obvious trap of being outraged by thinking this means "I am to blame for poor neurotransmission", we are left with a powerful sense of much more possibility of being able to influence this in some way. For anyone who 'has' depression, exposure to this first glimpse of knowledge that you can re-establish 'control' in your life can be one of the most extraordinary moments of realisation, of freedom and a renewed sense of optimism about the future. This renewed sense of possibility and hopefulness naturally starts to disrupt those patterns of depression listed at the beginning of this chapter.

If you are someone with experience of depression this may sound unreasonably easy, but having observed this moment of transition many thousands of times I can assure you it occurs just this way. The reason for such rapid change lies in the process of neuroplasticity discussed earlier and is due to one classically over-looked fact: People **dûing** depression are already very familiar with the fact that the brain changes very quickly. If you were to question them you would discover that at the start of 'the depression' the 'bleak thoughts' became very suddenly established at the expense of extinguishing the patterns of happiness.

Therefore it seems quite reasonable that if a process of neurological change has already been effective at completely changing the way a person viewed the world once before, then it's unsurprising that they could use exactly the same change process to see the world differently, again. The only difference is that in this case it is those 'depression patterns' that become destabilised, being rapidly replaced by the brilliant idea of a positive future, which then becomes self-fulfilling.

The more medically minded amongst you might now be considering if this could be applied to physical illnesses that affect or are caused by neurotransmission issues.

In the next chapter we will consider exactly those questions, but for now let's continue looking at happy, healthy brains.

Anxiety

Now that we've looked at depression it should be little surprise that we turn to its partner in crime, anxiety, which is similarly responsible for so many GPs' consultations and so much devastation of happiness.

Anxiety has a similar set of ways of looking at the world to depression, except with a slightly different focus. In anxiety the spotlight is mainly on what is about to go wrong, and on recognising that no matter what we do, it will.

Having seen the use of active and passives in depression we can fairly quickly apply the same ideas to anxiety.

If we take a core statement of anxiety:

"I am stressed."

and apply our tool kit from Chapter 8:

Passive Checklist

Signs	Details
1. "I feel"	
2. "I have"	
3. "I am"	I am
4. "It just is"	(It is just the way I am)
5. "They are"	
6. "I can't"	
7. "I get"	
8. "Made me"	
9. Obvious Passives	
10. Stuck	Yes
11. Moody, Stressed, Unhappy	Stressed
12. No sense of humour	Absent

Based on this checklist this is clearly showing up as using the Passive Perspective.

Clarity

Again using the 'Problems and Suggested Solutions' and 'Accuracy Question' we can become even clearer about whether the Passive Perspective has been used in a reasonable way or has been misused (Passive Language).

Just like with depression we can see that the way the phrase has been set up puts us in a very passive position as our main option is having to deal with **it** in someway (fight it, cope with it, wait for it to go, etc.) However if we look at the word anxiety we can see that it can't be put in a wheelbarrow, and so it is actually a nominalisation, not a noun. This means that anxiety isn't actually an 'it' or a 'thing'. So when we try and 'fight it' we discover that the thing we are trying to fight doesn't actually exist as a 'thing', and so fighting it is not an appropriate approach.

Actually what <u>can</u> I influence here?
Clearly the person you have the biggest influence over is you and, in this situation, the thing you need to have the most influence over is the way you are currently experiencing (and, we could say, choosing, albeit unconsciously, to see) the world.

So, once again we can confirm that this is an example of Passive Language, which means it's time to convert the passive into the active.

Converting it into Active Language, using dû
By inserting **dû** the sentence becomes simply:

"I **dû** stress."

If we use a more complex statement:

"When I see the untidy rooms in my house it makes me stressed."

This too shows up as Passive Language.

By splitting it into two and inserting the **dû** word the sentence becomes:

"I see the rooms are untidy in my house."

and

"I **dû** stress about it."

Once again don't be surprised if these phrases sounds very strange, it should do. It is unlikely that you will have ever heard someone say this before.

If you were the person with anxiety and you heard yourself saying "I am stressed" and used the techniques to change it to "I am **dûing** stress", then, remembering the discussion about Influence and blame covered previously, how does saying it in that way suddenly make you feel different?

This identification of choice and influence, and the separation of the house and the stress in the second example, suddenly provides us with a chance to make a different set of choices. Choices that don't involve thinking about the world in a stressful way. If you take this path just imagine what a relief it would be to no longer **dû** stress about such things.

Exercise 13.1
Is there ever a useful time to get stressed?

Did stress ever help?

Would there have been a better way to get what you wanted?

The chances are that wherever you got stressed it made things worse, or if it did get you what you wanted, there would have been a better way to get it.

Getting stressed about a untidy house and shouting at everyone or crying may get attention or even some house cleaning action, but how do you feel about yourself afterwards? Happy, or cross with yourself for not being able to deal with the situation in the way you wanted to? Would you have preferred to have motivated people to clean up their mess in a more calm fashion?

Does getting stressed about a taxi not coming to pick you up on time, or a deliveryman not bringing a delivery on the day they had arranged to help? Is there another way?

Stress is a very active body process, as those of us who've been stressed from time to time (that's everyone I've ever met, including me) can agree. Powerful sets of hormones (including Adrenaline, Noradrenaline, Cortisol, Dopamine and DHEA (Dehydroepiandrosterone) - which is a building block of sex hormones) are released into your bloodstream, they can cause your heart to beat faster, your breathing to change, your body temperature to increase or decrease, your head might spin or swim, your tummy may lurch or cramp, your immune system is affected, etc.

Unfortunately the stress response has its own vicious circle:

- You worry/anticipate stress.
- You produce the hormones of stress.
- They affect the body systems listed above.
- This produces strong, strange symptoms.
- You feel out of control.
- This makes you worried, and stressed.

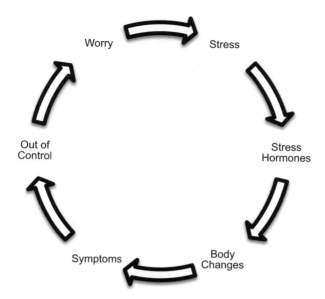

Again once when you become aware of your role in maintaining this and decide not to **dû** that anymore, the cycle collapses:

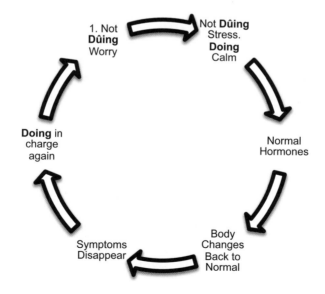

When put like this it seems simple, and actually it is. The only unfamiliar bit is to get to the understanding that you are **dûing** it without **dûing** blame about it, which you should be able to do now that you've read this book, and then, of course, to remember to use that Active Language even when the taxi is late, the house is untidy or you are waiting for an interview…

Will it be familiar? Not at first

Will it be life changing? Yes

Will become easier and more familiar with practise? Definitely

Have thousands of others applied these principles and changed their lives for the better forever? Absolutely

Other Uses
So if the secret to not being stressed is to not **dû** stress, and the secret to not being depressed is to not **dû** depressed, then what else can we apply this to?

Cautiously my team and I have been considering this question for some years and to date we have had equally amazing success in considering all sorts of common unhappiness/mental health issues in this way. The following list gives you some idea of the range of issues people have successfully applied this approach to. One of the issues in mental health that I would not currently recommend this approach for is anything where there is an 'altered reality'. That is where someone's reality seems at odds with or quite different from everyone else's, this is technically called psychosis. To give you some idea of when someone's reality is at odds with everyone else's, a simple example would be believing that there were little orange people everywhere telling you to do things, but no one else could see them. My experience is that when people with such altered realities consider the book's concepts, it is not that it has a negative impact on them, just that it doesn't make much sense to them.

However if, like the vast majority of people, your issues fit more into the list below this approach may be of great use to you.

Again whilst reading the list remember this is all about recognising you have an influence and can change and has nothing to do with blaming anyone for the way things have turned out so far:

- Obsessive Compulsive Disorder (OCD)/recurrent thoughts
- Depression/Sadness
- Anxiety/Fear/Stress
- Generalised Anxiety Disorder
- Bi-polar/Manic depression
- Guilt
- Phobias
- Social anxiety/phobia
- Shyness
- Lack of self-esteem/confidence
- Body Dysmorphic Disorder
- Anorexia/Bulimia

I would not necessarily recommend simply using this book as the complete way to resolve these things yourself although it will be very effective for many common daily issues. Some of these are quite complex issues and will need more guidance than can be gained simply by reading a book such as this. Instead I would consider this book as a useful stepping-stone to seeing things in a new light and to move from wherever you are to being ready to take one of our programmes.

Having looked at healthy, happy brains, it's naturally time to consider the applications of this approach in the body, and to look at physical health.

14. Physical Health

"Did you in any of your travels ever happen upon the Enchanted Acorn?" asked the piggy excitedly.

"Why, yes I did" replied the seasoned raconteur "but it is not anything like the way you might imagine it to be. And although it does exist, it is in fact not an acorn, nor something you can see or touch, as it is not so much a thing as a..."

Keen students of philosophy amongst you will have noticed that this chapter, looking at physical health and the last one, which discussed 'mental health', have been separated from each other on purpose. This has much to do with the lasting influence of a brilliant French mathematician and philosopher called Rene Descartes. To understand the potential impact on physical health that our new 'dûing' verb might have, it's important to first look at his contribution to the current world view of health issues and health care.

Descartes
Descartes musings on the nature of reality, although continuing on from the ideas of Plato and Aristotle,

started a whole new way of thinking, the effects of which have dominated western thought and science ever since.

Descartes had many ideas but his most well known are those which stemmed from his decision to call into question everything he believed, in order to find out what he was certain of.

The result of this was that he realised he could doubt whether his body was actually real (it could all be a dream, for example), but he couldn't doubt that he had a mind (his widely quoted "I think, therefore I am"). This in part persuaded him to consider the mind and body (which includes the physical brain) to be separate types of things in that:

1. The mind has no material substance (it doesn't take up any space, have any volume, length or weight, etc.)
2. The body has, more obviously, material substance (takes up space, has volume, length, weight, etc.)

This idea that these two fundamental components of us exist and are different in their nature is known as *dualism* (duo from the Latin for two).

Confusion in Science

Modern science has largely moved away from the theory of dualism and now favours a theory that everything can be explained in terms of a few fundamental physical laws (this theory is called *physicalist* or *physical monism*) - so the mental process/the mind can be explained in terms of chemical reactions which are physical and understandable. However in spite of this shift away from dualism, Descartes' idea of the separation of the human into the mind and the body still continues to hold much power and influence in science.

This is partly because when studying humans, science generally finds it easier to work with things that obey established scientific laws, like the body's chemicals, and it finds it less easy to get to grips with how the way we think might affect our body. One of the main reasons for this, as we now know, is that thoughts, which are the main currency of the mind, are nominalisations rather than nouns; they are processes rather than things. This makes them rather troublesome to study as they are difficult to measure, standardise, remove, dissect, stain with blue dyes or follow with radioactive markers, and so it makes it difficult to attribute or assess any changes in the body that might be caused by them.

This also highlights the fact that science, and especially medical science, is trying to juggle a number of differing and opposing ways of thinking, which just don't sit very well together. On one hand we have the *physicalist or 'Lego brick'* perspective, which suggests you can explain everything in terms of simpler systems. Much like in the world of Lego, everything can be made out of Lego bricks, you just need to have enough of them and fit them together in the right ways to make more and more complex things. This philosophy includes the perspective that the mind doesn't actually exist as separate entity from the body, that it is only a result of some basic chemical reactions. Aligned to this to a large degree is the widespread scientific argument that 'the mind can not influence the body'. However, this argument, or as the French philosopher Michel Focault (Foucault, 1969) would call it 'the discourse', raises interesting issues. Foucault would point out that engaging in this argument involving 'the mind' and 'the body' actually distinguishes the mind and the body as separate to each other, thereby encouraging the idea of dualism, which runs completely in opposition to the physicalist argument.

One of the problems that probably fuels this entire argument is the lack of definition of the word 'mind', very possibly because it is a nominalisation of a process rather than a noun. It is also not clear if there is a difference between soul, spirit and 'the mind' or if 'the mind' means the personality, the person's identity, their conscious or unconscious or even just the rational thinking functions of their brain - no wonder there is such confusion.

Science very reasonably likes to observe concrete connections between things to be certain that one is in someway linked to the other, to move from a hypothesis to an observed truth or fact. Seeing a bug directly causing a disease, or a chemical released at a synapse causing nerve transmission are good examples. But how do you observe something you can't see or detect like 'the mind' interacting with cells, when 'the mind' doesn't have substance, as it's not a 'thing'?

One of the leading researchers in the field of mind body medicine, the brilliant Ellen Langer describes her journey through this conflicting landscape. She was researching into the effect encouraging people in a nursing home to make more decisions for themselves, such as choosing where to receive visitors, and if and when to watch the movies that were shown at the home. She writes:

"...we were surprised, however, that (eighteen months later) less than half as many of the more

engaged group had died than had those in the control group.

I began to realize that ideas about mind/body dualism were just that, ideas, and a different, nondualist view of the mind and the body could be more useful. If we put the mind and the body back together so that we are just one person again, then wherever we put the mind, we would also put the body. If the mind is in a truly healthy place, the body would be as well - and so we could change our physical health by changing our minds." (Langer, 2009)

Interestingly Descartes himself writes about how much he recognised the mind (although a possibly more accurate translation of the word he actually used *'ame'* is the soul (Moerman, 2002)) clearly affected the body and the body affected the mind (known as *interactionism*), but he couldn't make sense of why that was when it seemed that they were made up of and existed in entirely different natures.

Whilst it is true that Descartes had some other ideas that have been generally ignored (such as the pineal gland being the location of the soul) it seems strange that the ideas of how the mind and body interact have been mainly lost whilst the focus has been so strong on the statements he made about the difference between mind and body.

Coming back to the starting point of this chapter you might wonder why I decided to keep these chapters on mind and body separate, because as you might have guessed, I personally consider the mind and body to be an integrated whole. This separation of chapters has been kept simply to make it an easier read for most people who have been brought up in a society which seems to consider these areas of health to be different or completely unrelated. However, you may have noticed I used the phrase *'seem* to consider these areas as unrelated' as there is another important area to explore which further highlights medical science's intriguing and confused relationship with the importance of mind and body interaction, the subject of 'placebos'.

Placebos

In medical research any new treatment approach needs to be tested (on a test group) and compared to what would happen if you didn't do anything at all (called the control group). However if the people in the group testing the new medicine got a pill to take but the ones in the control group weren't given any pills then there would be serious concerns about the validity of the results. This is because the test group would have known they were getting the new pill, the control group would have known they weren't getting any of the new medicine and the researchers would know who was getting the new drug and who wasn't.

To avoid this problem the control group are given some kind of apparently identical pill/treatment, but one that has no active or therapeutic ingredient. This pretend treatment is called a dummy or placebo.

Giving the placebo to the control group, and seeing how much they respond to the dummy pill then allows us to compare how much change the test group got compared to the placebo group and so work out how much change is due to the medicine and how much is due to the fact that we have just given them a pill.

This all sounds quite reasonable and straightforward until you pause for a moment and consider why the placebos are needed in the first place.

Keeping in mind the idea that the placebos are needed in order to eliminate any response due to just giving a pill, whether inert or real raises a very interesting fact. It tells us that researchers know that some of the effect of giving a pill is not due to anything in the pill - the 'placebo effect' - but how does that work?

Exactly the same reasoning is behind the arrangements in a double blind control trial (the most common method for testing the effectiveness of drugs). In these trials neither the subjects of the experiments or the people handing out the pills know which is a genuine medication and which is a dummy, because it appears that even the person handing out the pills can have an influence on the way the person responds to taking it.

So how can a pill with nothing in it actually influence our body's chemistry? How can we explain the fact that if the person handing out the pill knows whether the pill is real or fake it will make a difference to the physiology of person who is taking it?

Clearly this is a brilliant example of the way our thoughts have the ability to influence our physiology. Medical science recognises this as such an issue that could interfere with the accuracy of results that every day thousands of people are testing drugs against the power of the placebo effect. And almost without recognising it, on each occasion medical science reconfirms its position that the mind does after all influence the body.

The medical anthropologist Daniel Moerman has written a brilliant book considering the placebo effect (Moerman, 2002). In it he explores the wealth of scientific data to support the idea that taking an inactive dummy pill does have a profound effect on our bodies and that there is an abundance of data to reference as every drug has to be tested against a placebo. He also argues for a new understanding of the placebo effect, which he suggests is given a new and more useful title, the 'meaning response', suggesting that it is not the placebo that causes the effect but our interpretation of what taking that pill/treatment means to us.

> *"...the meaning response...is...the psychological and physiological effects of meaning in the treatment of illness."*

Placebos have traditionally been a considered in medicine and medical science as a short hand for pretence, gullibility and quackery (Moerman, 2002). Often summed up with the idea that "oh, that treatment only works through the placebo effect". As a result much of scientific research asks how the annoying placebo effect can be eliminated from messing up the experiments and ruining the statistics.

However if we examine some of the many examples of responses to placebos, we might also start to think about placebos in a new light:

Ulcers:
Dr Lanza's (Lanza F., 1994) experiment to test two drugs for stomach ulcers showed that after two weeks of taking the drugs 30% of the subjects showed improvement when their stomach wall was viewed with an endoscope.

At four weeks 66% of those on Xantac and 88% on Prevacid had healed ulcers - good news for the makers of Prevacid.

But there was also a control group of people with ulcers who as part of the study were given placebos, although, naturally, they didn't know the pills were inert. At two weeks 33% of the subjects showed improvement when their stomach wall was viewed with an endoscope. At four weeks 43% had healed ulcers.

Colours:
Schapira et al (Schapira, McClelland, Griffiths, & Newell, 1970) found that people responded to the drug Oxazepam (a drug similar to Valium) differently depending on the colour of the pill. People with anxiety got better results with green pills, those with depression responded better to yellow ones.

Effect of advertising:
In an inspired and much cited experiment (Braithwaite & Cooper, 1981) a team considered the effects of painkillers on headaches. There were four different groups in the experiment, all of whom thought they were receiving painkillers to help with headaches. The groups were divided as below, receiving different versions of the painkillers:

Group 1: Their painkillers were simply labelled as unbranded 'analgesic tablets' - but were actually a placebo

Group 2: Their painkillers were boxed and branded exactly like a well known and well advertised pain killer - but were actually a placebo

Group 3: Their painkillers were simply labelled as unbranded 'analgesic tablets' - but was actually the well known and well advertised pain killer

Group 4: Their painkillers were boxed and branded exactly like a well-known and well advertised pain killer - which they actually were!

When the results were analysed they showed the real painkiller (groups 3 and 4) was better than the placebo (groups 1 and 2), but it also showed the 'branded' placebo (group 2) was better than the unbranded one (group 1) and the 'branded 'painkiller (group 4) was better than the identical pill when packaged to look unbranded (group 3).

Astrological Beliefs
In a study by D. P. Phillips, from the University of California, the effect of beliefs amongst the Chinese American community about the health effects of being born in a certain astrological year were compared to a group of non Chinese-Americans. Although this is not a classical study about placebos versus treatment it raises the same issues in an even larger context.

> *"We examined the deaths of 28,169 adult Chinese-Americans, and 412,632 randomly selected, matched controls coded "white" on the death certificate. Chinese-Americans, but not whites, die significantly earlier than normal (1.3-4.9 years) if they have a combination of disease and birth-year which Chinese astrology and medicine consider ill-fated. The more strongly a group is attached to Chinese traditions, the more years of life are lost. Our results hold for nearly all major causes of death studied. The reduction in survival cannot be*

completely explained by a change in the behaviour of the Chinese patient, doctor, or death-registrar, but seems to result at least partly from psychosomatic processes."

Moerman's perspective together with results such as the intriguing ones above, move the debate on from the idea of the placebo effect being simply an annoyance and raises a much more interesting and important question which has taken up a large part of my last 25 years of professional practice and research.

Even the most basic appreciation of placebos shows us that we have an amazing ability to influence our healing systems to some extent or other (taking placebos can cause powerful negative side effects just like drugs too). I suggest this is something we should be amazed at rather than annoyed by and that we should consider, "How can we harness this ability of the body to change its health state independent of external drugs or treatment?"

Physical Health and Active Language
The slightly complex, and at times philosophical, start to this chapter has been an attempt to set the scene for what for some people can initially seem the most challenging application of the ideas of Passive and Active Language. In the introduction to this chapter I have hoped to induce some questioning of the widely held belief that whilst we may naturally find it easier to see 'mental issues' as being influenced by the mind we often hold that physical issues are just that - physical - and outside the mind's influence. From the scientifically collected evidence presented I hope you can see that the lines are no way as clear cut as many of us imagined, and this hopefully will give you flexibility in considering how language might affect our bodies.

Passive Patients

I have already covered this topic in some depth in other books, but I feel it's worth mentioning again especially in this context. The origin of the word *patient* comes from the Latin word *patiens*, meaning 'one who endures' or 'one who suffers'. Similarly the adjective patience means 'enduring trying circumstances with even temper'. This is of course also the root of the word passive. It seems that the ideas of being passive have been long linked to being ill and seeking help to recover. I suppose this is a relatively natural way to think about it, as when you have a broken leg you do need someone to fix it for you, or if you have a high fever and are confined to bed, you need people to look after you.

However there is still much action going on inside you which is central to your recovery. If you have a broken leg, the plaster cast will not mend your bones, it will only keep it straight and still whilst **you** heal and mend the break, and the people taking care of you whilst you are ill with a fever are playing a supportive role whilst **your** body fights off the infection.

There has been much interest in these ideas from medical circles, with some authorities (Neuberger, 1999) arguing that the term 'patient' should be dropped because it underlines the inferior status of recipients of health-care. For them, "The active patient is a contradiction in terms and it is the assumption underlying the passivity that is the most dangerous".

The other main word used in medicine and treatments instead of patient is *client*. But this also has some interesting historical meanings. Its Latin root *cliens* means 'one who is obliged to make supplications to a powerful figure for material assistance'. Once again this word creates a rather disempowering relationship between the person who is ill and the health provider.

So the two main words used to describe people with health issues have their origins in Passive Language - this tells us something of how long standing the idea of being passive has been associated with ideas of illness. Maybe it's time to reconsider if this is the best way to think about illness.

Physical Health as a Process
As we have already discussed in the earlier chapters on labelling and mental health there is good reason to consider physical health as a dynamic balancing act between:

The forces and agents which work to cause our tissues to breakdown (technically called entropy), including:

- Invading organisms
- Poison and chemical toxins (including the by-products of everyday cell function and food waste)
- Radiation
- Gravity, etc.

And those forces which counteract those sustained attacks:

- Healthy immune function
- Making good choices about our diet and exercise regime
- Getting enough sleep, etc.

In this vibrant tussle between our life support systems and the various factors that oppose them, the idea of being active and having an influence to some extent on that tussle seems not only biologically reasonable but also exciting.

In the examples of lateness, depression, upset and anxiety we've already seen the power of moving from a state of seemingly 'having no influence' over a situation to a state where we recognise that we do have a vital influence.

Now we will consider these ideas in relation to specific physical health conditions. I am not going to go into full details as to the complete approach to any and all physical illness in this book as it is simply not the right media to deal with such complex issues in; a book can guess at your questions and answer some of them but obviously you can't have a detailed interactive conversation with it. As every illness and every person needs to be considered as an individual case the correct forum for proper, personally tailored assistance is to visit an experienced practitioner in this field. What I hope you will get from this book is an idea of the possibilities of this language and the knowledge that others have already made positive and lasting changes in their health by applying these concepts.

Let's begin with looking at a very physical illness, Multiple Sclerosis.

Multiple Sclerosis
Over the last few years I started to receive inquiries from people with certain neurological issues, such as Multiple Sclerosis (MS), Cerebral Palsy and 'strokes', wanting to know if there was any possibility of an improvement in their health state by using the Lightning Process, a major element of which is the 'dûing' approach.

MS was one condition that especially interested me. One of the main diagnostic factors in diagnosing someone with MS is to identify the presence of the 'sclerotic lesions' (a scar on the nerve's coating, in very simple terms).

MS has a number of different 'types', one of these is the 'relapsing and remitting' type. In this type the symptoms get worse and better from time to time. In some cases the periods of wellness can last for years or even decades. Interestingly in those periods of wellness the 'sclerotic lesions' are still present - so under a microscope there are no detectable differences between the relapse and remission phases. So whilst they still have the lesions and are well, what else is going on, and is there anyway to extend these periods of wellness?

An interesting thing happens when we ask them, whilst they are in the remission stage, "Are you well or ill?"

It becomes clear that this is actually a very difficult question to answer; our normal language can't quite cope with this situation.

It's true they have multiple sclerotic lesions, and yes they have a propensity for it to return, but whilst they are in the remission/fully well phase are they ill?

Does it make better sense if we use Active Language (again remembering the in depth discussion on Influence and blame)? If we ask in the relapse or remission stage of the illness:

"Are you **dûing** the symptoms of MS?"

Then the answers, yes and no, have much more clarity than asking are you well or ill. In addition this new language encourages the sense that the illness is a process rather than a stuck thing. And as a process it has more of a sense of the possibility to change.

Just for complete clarity it's worth pointing out, again, this does not make it an unreal, pretend or an 'all in the mind' illness, it just redraws our attention to the active nature of the processes involved in the maintenance of the illness state. Once we get over the potential shock of putting it in such a strange way, this Active Language again allows for a recognition of the process that is occurring within the body. And with that comes a sense that there is some flexibility as to what might happen next and the possibility for change rather than stagnation.

It then becomes possible to have the lesions and "not **dû** MS symptoms" which is a good description of what is happening in the phases of wellness.

There is also the possibility of changing our perspective of the lesions as being static nouns that just 'are', to seeing them as an inflammatory 'process' within the neurological system. This shift naturally opens up the options of considering if there is anything that could be done to calm down, slow down or even stop this inflammatory response, or possibly reverse it altogether.

We don't yet know the answers to all these questions, but working from the position of considering "what if MS is something you **dû**?" then another question would naturally follow, "is there any way to not **dû** it as much?"

Here's a brief report from someone who decided to look at their MS in exactly this way, which at the very least is interesting food for thought:

P. was diagnosed with chronic progressive MS. After six years of the illness they were introduced to the concept of 'dûing' as part of a Lightning Process course. They found that by applying it they were able to significantly reduce their muscle pain and weakness, and their bladder and bowel symptoms and they now enjoy a much better quality of life.

A brief example of how to apply this change of language to affect physical symptoms follows. Please note that from the way it is written this may seem almost too easy an approach for something as complex as making a difference to neurological dysfunction. It's important to keep in mind that the description below is a very simplified version of what occurs, and doesn't really go into, in any depth, the profound change that is occurring across a range of physical body systems as a result of this perceptual and neurological shift.

On noticing muscle weakness whilst walking they might reasonably find themselves saying, "My muscles are weak". Using the dûing approach they would change the words to 'I am **dûing** weak muscles". Then using the strategy outlined in chapter 10 they would work out how they would like their muscles to feel (they would want them "to be strong") and use powerful memories of muscle strength to starting **'doing'** strong muscles.

This may, at first, seem like something that they would have no influence over, until you start to read the many scientific research papers on the linkage between the muscles and mental training. In one of these papers researchers compared three groups:

1.   The first group who exercised a particular muscle

2.   The second group who only practised mentally exercising that muscle
3.   The third group who didn't exercise that muscle at all

They found that subjects in group three showed no change; those in groups one and, more surprisingly, in group two found significant improvement in the strength of their muscles, so clearly we all do have a significant and measurable influence on our neuromuscular system. (Ranganathan, Siemionow, Liu, Sahgal, & Yue, 2004) (Jeannerod, 2005) (Sidaway B., 2005):

This person, P., with MS reported how, before learning and applying these ideas, their balance was poor and they were unable to walk more than 100 yards without a stick or assistance.

However after applying the idea of dûing their walking was noticeably steadier and they could walk up and down slopes. A few weeks later they found they could now walk energetically for over a mile and a half. Within a few months they could stand, confidently and without help.

Exactly how you might be able to achieve these kinds of changes by utilising the brain and body connection to assist your neurological and immune system to function in a more healthy way are well beyond the scope of this book.

Exercise 14.1
As an experiment, notice what happens when you take a health issue that affects you personally and apply Active Language to it. Please note that this is not saying you aren't ill and don't have an illness/recovery process going on inside of you, or that you should stop taking your

medicine, stop consulting your doctors or start ignoring their advice. But it is saying what role could you have in positively influencing your health. And not just from a "I'll stop smoking and do more exercise" perspective which would be an excellent start anyway - but asking in addition "how might I influence my whole body's response to this illness/recovery process?"

Final Thoughts

For some of you reading this section you might have found some of the ideas presented here quite a stretch to accept based on your experience or beliefs. I think I would have been feeling much the same if I hadn't been immersed in this field for some time. However, as the example given above is just one of a growing number of cases where major changes have been independently observed, it does raise some very interesting questions about how something as apparently abstract as language could potentially have such a powerful effect on our physical health. Could it be that language, an area we've never really considered to be a likely candidate for making a difference to health, might just be one of the key missing components to resolving a range of illnesses that are unresponsive to our current approaches?

15.   Conclusion

"...as a what?" asked the piggy excitedly "the acorn is a what?"

"Well, just as I said to the three billy-goat-gruffs when they employed me as a management consultant for their relocation project. Whatever you do, whichever journeys you embark upon in life there will always be rivers and bridges to cross. And there will always, somewhere in that journey, be trolls. But most of the trolls are in here and here" he said, pointing to his head and his heart, "and those are the ones that you really need to deal with."

"And when you have", continued the wise old spider "then you will discover the Enchanted Acorn was something within *every one of us that is always there, we just need to remember to look for it."*

And with that he winked, turned and faded back into the forest. Somewhere in the distance a clock chimed. Twelve strikes rang out for midnight.

I hope you have enjoyed this philosophical journey through my ideas on the power of language and how it can be used as both a tool to identify where we are getting ourselves into trouble and how we can recognise those traps and free ourselves. It may be worth, as with many a journey's end spending a few moments reflecting, reviewing the important points before, hopefully starting to use this voyage and its discoveries as a compass for a brilliant future.

Summary

We began sometime ago at the start of this journey, explaining that new ideas that challenge the old order can take a while to become accepted.

We explored the urban jungle of Negative Wants, both obvious and Hidden, and the more sinister and shadowy inhabitants of Language Patterns. We paid special attention to the troublesome issue of Passive Language which had a brilliant disguise of appearing perfectly normal whilst actually being behind some of the most extreme forms of stuckness known to man.

We started to recognise how disempowering Passive Language was, how we could spot it and change it into Active Language. We noticed how strange the sound of Active Language was and how that strangeness assisted the sense of how powerful you could be in those situations.

Finally we began to expand on how it might be possible to apply these ideas not just to everyday experiences but also to mental and physical health issues.

Any journey should leave you changed by the experience; I hope this one has been thought provoking and useful. Knowing what amazing and profound change others have achieved by applying these concepts to their lives, I can only hope that something of a similar and wonderful nature begins to unfold in yours, so that you can have - sorry, **do** - a great life.

Edûcation

Many people who have learnt to use dû and find how much it can change one's life and perspective have asked me an interesting and important question; "Why weren't we taught this when we were learning to speak, and when will this be taught to everyone?"

If the book has managed to adequately explain the potential of dû to you then I hope you will see what possibility they are considering; that of everyone knowing about personal influence; of a situation where we all recognise when we are genuinely passive to something and when we are talking ourselves out of being powerful without even knowing it. "What if", they often ask, "the whole world knew this; if it were taught in schools along with the other verbs? What then? Where if the phrase 'he made me angry' didn't work in playgrounds, offices or marriages any more and was replaced with an understanding that 'they did something' and 'I responded to it in a way I'd rather not'? Surely that would move us towards a world of naturally increased choices, and chances for clear communication and increased happiness?"

It's certainly something I'd like to see; and wouldn't it be strange for that change to occur from a change in our use of grammar, just by using a new verb.

Duing.org

I've set up this website to keep you up to date with the developments of the dû, and to provide a place to meet and interact with other pioneers who are starting to use it in their lives. Unfortunately the internet doesn't dû web addresses with û's in them yet (although I might have a word with Sir Tim Berners Lee about that!). It's also designed to be a useful starting point for those unfamiliar with the dû, so let your friends know.

I'd like to finish with some other people's words:

> *"The human mind treats a new idea the same way the body treats a strange protein; it rejects it."* - P.B. Medawar

> *"Man's mind, once stretched by a new idea, never regains its original dimensions."* - Oliver Wendell Holmes

> *"An invasion of armies can be resisted, but not an idea whose time has come."* - Victor Hugo

> *"I can't understand why people are frightened of new ideas. I'm frightened of the old ones."* - John Cage

Answers to Chapter 10

In Chapter 10, I presented some statements to apply your new skills to; here are some of the possible answers.

1. "I feel angry about the way my parents treat me."

Spotting Passives

Again we need to start by spotting the passives. Use the checklist below as before.

Passive Checklist

Signs	Details
1. "I feel"	I feel
2. "I have"	
3. "I am"	
4. "It just is"	
5. "They are"	(They are treating me badly)
6. "I can't"	
7. "I get"	
8. "Made me"	(My parents make me angry)
9. Obvious Passives	My feelings depend on something I can't control
10. Stuck	I'm a victim of the way they treat me
11. Moody, Stressed, Unhappy	Yes
12. No sense of humour	Absent

Clarity

Problem: Parents' behaviour.

Solution: They need to change.

Accuracy: Are they puppeteers?

Actually, what <u>can</u> I influence here?

You can't change your parents, but you can, of course, change how you deal with the parent's behaviours. You shouldn't *have* to do this, of course, but if you want to make a change, then you are the one who will have to change.

Converting this into Active Language, using dû

"My parents treat me in a particular way."

and

"I **dû** anger about it."

Maybe it's time to not **dû** that anymore?

2. "I try not to be late, but I have difficulty with being on time."

Spotting Passives

Again we need to start by spotting the passives. Use the checklist below as before.

Passive Checklist

Signs	Details
1. "I feel"	
2. "I have"	I have
3. "I am"	
4. "It just is"	
5. "They are"	
6. "I can't"	
7. "I get"	
8. "Made me"	
9. Obvious Passives	I can't do anything about my lateness
10. Stuck	I'm a victim of the way I am
11. Moody, Stressed, Unhappy	
12. No sense of humour	

Clarity

Problem: I have a difficulty with time-keeping which is just part of who I am.

Solution: People need to accommodate my lateness.

Accuracy: Is it really out of your control, have you never been on time?

Actually, what <u>can</u> I influence here?
See the section on lateness in Chapter 5. Maybe you could leave earlier and plan better?

Converting this into Active Language, using 'dû'
By inserting **dû,** the sentence becomes:

"I try not to be late."

and

"I **dû** difficulty with being on time."

"I **dû** making sure I am late"

3. "I am bad with new people."

Spotting Passives
Again we need to start by spotting the passives. Use the checklist below as before.

Passive Checklist

Signs	Details
1. "I feel"	
2. "I have"	
3. "I am"	I am
4. "It just is"	(It is just the way it is)
5. "They are"	
6. "I can't"	
7. "I get"	
8. "Made me"	(New people make me feel 'bad')
9. Obvious Passives	It's something I can't control
10. Stuck	Yes
11. Moody, Stressed, Unhappy	Unhappy around new people
12. No sense of humour	Absent

Clarity
Problem: Meeting new people.

Solution: Avoid meeting new people.

Accuracy: Are those new people puppeteers, who are able to make you feel things?

Actually, what <u>can</u> I influence here?
You can't change the new people, or the fact that there will be new people appearing at various points in your life, but you can of course change how you deal with those situations.

Converting this into Active Language, using dû

By inserting **dû,** the sentence becomes:

"There are new people to meet."

and

"I **dû** 'bad' about it."

or

"I **dû** feeling bad about it."

4. "It's always been the same, I am shy. It just is the way I am."

Spotting Passives

Again we need to start by spotting the passives. Use the checklist below as before.

Passive Checklist

Signs	Details
1. "I feel"	
2. "I have"	
3. "I am"	I am
4. "It just is"	It is just the way it is
5. "They are"	
6. "I can't"	
7. "I get"	
8. "Made me"	(People make me feel shy)
9. Obvious Passives	It's something I can't control
10. Stuck	Shy
11. Moody, Stressed, Unhappy	Unhappy around social situations
12. No sense of humour	Absent

Clarity

Problem: I have the shyness gene; I have no choice but to be shy.

Solution: Avoid social situations, or put up with it.

Accuracy: Are there some people who used to be shy and now aren't? Are you shy with your closest friends and family?

Actually, what <u>can</u> I influence here?
You can't always avoid social situations throughout your entire life, but you can of course change how you deal with those situations.

Converting this into Active Language, using dû
This is a very simple statement that really only has one part "I am shy", which is repeated a few times. By inserting **dû,** the sentence becomes:

"I **dû** shyness really well and have done for a long time."

5. "I am just one of those people who can't understand maths."

Spotting Passives

Again we need to start by spotting the passives. Use the checklist below as before.

Passive Checklist

Signs	Details
1. "I feel"	
2. "I have"	
3. "I am"	I am
4. "It just is"	(It is just the way it is)
5. "They are"	
6. "I can't"	I can't
7. "I get"	
8. "Made me"	
9. Obvious Passives	It's something I can't control
10. Stuck	Yes
11. Moody, Stressed, Unhappy	Unhappy around maths
12. No sense of humour	Absent

Clarity

Problem: I don't have the maths gene; I have no choice but to be bad at maths.

Solution: Avoid maths.

Accuracy: Are there some people who used to be bad at maths and now aren't? Are you bad with all maths, can you tell the difference between $1 and $1000,000? Can you work out how many fingers you have?

Actually, what <u>can</u> I influence here?
The way I approach maths.

Converting this into Active Language, using dû
Again this is a very simple statement that really only has one part "I can't understand maths". By inserting **dû,** the sentence becomes:

"I **dû** 'not understanding maths' really well and have done for a long time."

or

"I **dû** 'maths is difficult'."

or

"I **dû** scared and confused about maths."

And suddenly the options for sorting this out seem much simpler and possible.

6. "I get stressed."

Spotting Passives
Again we need to start by spotting the passives. Use the checklist below as before.

Passive Checklist

Signs	Details
1. "I feel"	
2. "I have"	
3. "I am"	
4. "It just is"	(It is just the way it is)
5. "They are"	
6. "I can't"	
7. "I get"	I get
8. "Made me"	
9. Obvious Passives	It's something I can't control
10. Stuck	Stressed
11. Moody, Stressed, Unhappy	Stressed
12. No sense of humour	Absent

Clarity
Problem: I get stressed and I have no choice.

Solution: Avoid anything that might make you stressed, feel stressed all the time, or look for medication to sedate yourself.

Accuracy: Do you get stressed all the time? Can you be calm sometimes too? Are there some people who used to be as stressed as you are and now aren't?

Actually, what can I influence here?
The way I approach life.

Converting this into Active Language, using dû

Again this is a very simple statement that really only has one part "I get stressed". By inserting **dû,** the sentence becomes:

"I **dû** 'stress' really well and have done for a long time."

Once we recognise that *we* are **dûing** stress then we automatically feel a reduction in the sense of lack of control in our lives, which in turn reduces our stress. It opens up the possibility that if we have been **dûing** stress we could also learn to not **dû** it, which makes us less stressed about our future.

7. "What she said made me feel fat."

Spotting Passives
Again we need to start by spotting the passives. Use the checklist below as before.

Passive Checklist

Signs	Details
1. "I feel"	I feel flat
2. "I have"	
3. "I am"	
4. "It just is"	
5. "They are"	
6. "I can't"	
7. "I get"	
8. "Made me"	Her words made me
9. Obvious Passives	It's something I can't control
10. Stuck	Yes
11. Moody, Stressed, Unhappy	Unhappy
12. No sense of humour	Absent

Clarity
Problem: She said something and I had no choice but to feel 'bad'/fat.

Solution: Diet, be upset, or get revenge.

Accuracy: Can people really make you feel something like 'upset'? (This is the puppeteer argument again.)

Actually, what <u>can</u> I influence here?
The way you deal with what she said.

Converting this into Active Language, using dû
By inserting **dû,** the sentence becomes:

"She said something."

and

"I **dîd** 'feeling fat'."

or

"I **dîd** 'taking it to heart/believing her'."

Once we recognise that the two things are not directly linked in the way we have stated and we don't have to **dû** 'feeling fat' just because of someone's unpleasantness, we can start to change how we feel about ourselves. When we change from **dûing** self hatred to doing self love, we are much more likely be motivated to make the changes we need to get the life we want.

The Fairy Tale

A number of people who read the book before it was published loved the fairy tale as a story in it's own right and asked me if I could include it, in it's entirety here at the end of the book. So if you're sitting comfortably, I'll begin...

Once upon a time there were three little piggies; the cleverest, brightest eyed piggies you ever did see; all day long they snuffled and oinked happily, as they dug for acorns and truffles in the sunshine - until one Wednesday, at the height of summer, just on the stroke of midnight...

...for on that Wednesday night, just on the stroke of midnight, one of the piggies woke up with a start and realised that something was very different. He sniffed the air, and there was no denying it - the beautiful scent of the Enchanted Acorn was drifting on the breeze. Legend had it, as every young piggy in the world knew, that a piggy could find the secret of contentment once they dug up the Enchanted Acorn. The piggy woke up his friends, but even before they stretched, yawned and grumpily rubbed their eyes, the scent had disappeared, like mist in a forest.

Maybe, they suggested, the piggy had been dreaming, maybe he should stop thinking about the Enchanted Acorn and that fairy story for babies, and maybe he should eat less cheese before bed and keep his late night delusions to himself...

...he tried to snuggle back down to sleep but a small whisper of a voice seemed to keep jolting him out of his

sleepiness. Following the sound he trotted out of the door and into the dark, dark forest night.

The sound became clearer as he entered the very deepest part of the forest, he could make it out more now, the tiny voice spoke with a certain kind of a rhythm, and it sounded eversomuch like someone practising spells…

…rounding a huge gnarled tree, he stumbled upon a tiny, brightly coloured elf, who seeming as surprised as he, stepped back in shock, and as she did so she became tangled up into a huge spider's web. The more she wriggled the more she became stuck fast…

…"Help, help, there is no way out!" she yelled, rousing a sleeping shape who moved slowly and ominously towards her...

…she knew with absolute certainty she was in trouble. Trapped, and at the mercy of the worryingly dark shape that moved menacingly towards her. The more she twisted and turned the more she realised how completely trapped she was. No good could come of this.

Something about this reminded the piggy of when he had tried to take his new Ikea sofa upstairs. At the turn of the stairs, the sofa became stuck fast and would go no further no matter how hard he pushed and pulled…

…leaving the sofa in the stairway seemed the only option. For a few days the piggies climbed over or around it each time they went downstairs to the kitchen to make a cauldron of soup, in case a wolf came a calling again, or sighed with annoyance as they climbed upstairs to bed…

...what was it, thought the piggy, about this elf being tangled in a web, that so reminded him of the stuck sofa?...

...then he remembered. In a moment of brilliance worthy of his two heroes, the wisest of all pigs, Einstyn and Nils Boar, he had realised that if the sofa can become stuck, then logically if you reverse the pathway that lead to it becoming stuck you can make it unstuck. He shouted to the elf to stop wriggling and to start behaving like his sofa...

...as if by magic, the simple advice seemed to work, as she retraced her movements the web fell away from her, and she was free...

...although she was now free, the dark shape that crouched near the web moved towards her...

..."I am so sorry", exclaimed the embarrassed laundry spider. "I really should have taken my washing line down last night, but friends came round with some whiskey and cards and we, well we played poker all night and I fell asleep. I am so sorry. If there is anything I can do to make amends, please do let me know."...

...the piggy and the elf were taken aback to find how delightful and well mannered their new friend the laundry owner was. It seemed he had had a life where he was determined to have seized every opportunity that came his way and to relish all life had to offer. And any fear they had had completely vanished as he began to tell extraordinary tales of the people he had met and the sights he had seen whilst on tour with the rock band 'The Spiders from Mars'...

"Did you in any of your travels ever happen upon the Enchanted Acorn?" asked the piggy excitedly.

"Why, yes I did" replied the seasoned raconteur "but it is not anything like the way you might imagine it to be. And although it does exist, it is in fact not an acorn, nor something you can see or touch, as it is not so much a thing as a…"

"…as a what?" asked the piggy excitedly "the acorn is a what?"

"Well, just as I said to the three billy-goats-gruff when they employed me as a management consultant for their relocation project. Whatever you do, whichever journeys you embark upon in life there will always be rivers and bridges to cross. And there will always, somewhere in that journey, be trolls. But most of the trolls are in here and here" he said, pointing to his head and his heart, "and those are the ones that you really need to deal with."

"And when you have", continued the wise old spider "then you will discover the Enchanted Acorn was something within every one of us that is always there, we just need to remember to look for it."

And with that he winked, turned and faded back into the forest. Somewhere in the distance a clock chimed. Twelve strikes rang out for midnight.

Glossary

There are a number of quite technical and often new linguistic terms used throughout the book, this brief guide should help to make these words more familiar to you.

Active Language: This is used to describe a situation where you feel you have options, that you can change things and that you can take action to improve how a situation turns out or how you feel about it. It is the opposite of feeling passive in a situation.

Closed Questions: These are questions that limit the possible answers available. An example is "Do you drink between 1 and 5 units of alcohol a week, or more than 5 units a week?" The possible answers are only 'between 1 and 5' and 'over 5'. The question has effectively removed '0' as an option.

Facts: Facts, unlike opinions and beliefs, are just data. They are pieces of information that can be verified independently of the person who presents them.

Hidden Negatives: These are words that sound like they are bursting with positivity, pointing us towards what we wish for in our lives. On closer inspection we find that they are actually negatives, reminding us of exactly what we don't want.

I want to be brave. You would only need to be brave if you were facing something that you felt fearful about.

"I am going to be brave and sit down" means there is something you are a bit concerned about that might happen if you sit down.

Influence: This is the ability to make a difference to something. So 'having an influence' means being someone who is going to do something about resolving a situation, by recognising the elements they can influence and then affecting those things to make a difference.

Language Patterns: These are patterns than can be recognised in the way people talk. In this book two main patterns are discussed; Active and Passive Language patterns.

Negative Wants: This is a common way of speaking where we express what we want by talking about what we don't want, e.g. "I want to not be anxious".

Nominalisations: This is where a process or an action (a verb) has been changed into a noun. 'He was dancing' becomes 'we saw a dance'. This creates a sense that 'the dance' is an object, a noun, something that has substance and exists as a thing. But it's not, as it fails the simple wheelbarrow test (can you put it in a wheelbarrow?).

Nouns: These are 'object' words, used to describe things, people or places.

Opinions/beliefs: These two should be considered as the same thing. They are a view, conviction or perspective that is held by one person or more; but they are not necessarily facts. That is because they are not based on unbiased evidence; they are based on judgements, guesses or approximations.

Paradigm/Paradigm shift: A paradigm is used to describe a way of looking at things - especially one that is generally accepted to be true. A good example of a paradigm is the idea that 'the earth is the centre of the universe'. There was a long period of history where this was thought to be true, and this was the accepted model. In hindsight we can see now it was wrong and it was just a generally held belief - a paradigm. A paradigm shift is when one of these well-accepted truths about the way things are is found out to be false, as a result, a large chunk of our knowledge, which was based on the false assumptions, has to be thrown out. We then have to start to work out what is now 'true' based on our new understandings.

Passives and the Passive Perspective: A description that we are powerless in a situation; one in which things are occurring that are beyond our control, e.g. "the weather was good/bad today". The weather is something we are powerless to control, therefore we are passive to it.

Passive Statements: This is the kind of language we use to describe situations in which we are genuinely passive.

The Passive Problem: This is when it appears to us that we are passive to a situation and powerless to change it - but we are mistaken. We do actually have some influence on the situation, but don't recognise that we do because we think we are passive in the situation.

Passive Language: This is when we use Passive Statements to describe a situation, e.g. "the weather made me depressed", but it is one of those occasions when we are mistaken. This implies that the weather has to change before our mood will lift, and we are passive until this happens. Once we identify that this is the misuse of Passive Language then we can use the new verb 'dû' to convert it into Active Language and rediscover other options.

Verbs: 'doing' or action words (he walks, we talked, she eats).

Bibliography

Baez, K., Aiarzaguena, J. M., Grandes, G., Pedrodo, E., Aranguren, J., & Retolaza, A. (1998). Understanding patient-initiated frequent attendance in primary care: case control study. *Br J Gen Pract , 48*, 1824–1827.

Bolstad, R. (2002). *RESOLVE.* Crown House Publishing.

Braithwaite, A., & Cooper, P. (1981). Analgesic effects of branding in treatment of headaches. *BMJ* (282), 1576–1578.

Foucault, M. (1969). *The Archaeology of Knowledge.* France: Éditions Gallimard.

Grinder, R., & Bandler, R. (1975). *Structure of Magic I.* Palo Alto: Science and Behaviour Books Inc.

Jankowsky, J., Melnikova, T., Fadale, D., Xu, G., Slunt, H., Gonzales, V., et al. (2005, May 25). Environmental enrichment mitigates cognitive deficits in a mouse model of Alzheimer's disease. *Journal of Neuroscience* , 5217-24.

Jeannerod, M. (2005). Mental imagery in the motor context. *Neuropsychologia, 33* (11), 1419-1432.

Kirsch, I., Deacon, B., Huedo-Medina, B., Scoboria, A., Moore, T., & Johnson, T. (2008). *Initial Severity and Antidepressant Benefits: A Meta-Analysis of Data Submitted to the Food and Drug Administration.* Public Library of Science.

Kuhn, T. (1962). *The Structure of Scientific Revolutions.* Chicago: University of Chicago Press.

Langer, E. (2009). *Counterclockwise: Mindful Health and the Power of Possibility.* Ballantine Books.

Lanza, F. (1994). Double-blind Comparison of Lansoprazole, Ranitidine, and Placebo in the Treatment of Acute Duodenal Ulcer. *The American Journal of Gastroenterology , 89* (8), 1191-1200.

Neal, R., Heywood, P., Morley, S., & al., e. (1998). Frequency of patients' consulting patterns in general practice and workload generated by frequent attenders: comparisons between practices. *Br J Gen Pract ; , 48,* 895–898.

Neuberger, J. (1999). Let's do away with patients. *BMJ* (318), 1756-8.

McFarland, B., Freeborn, D., Mullooly, J., & Pope, C. (1985). Utilization patterns among long-term enrolees in a prepaid group practice health maintenance organization. *Med Care , 23,* 1221–1233.

Moerman, D. (2002). *Meaning, Medicine and The 'Placebo Effect'.* Cambridge: Cambrdge University Press.

Ranganathan, V. K., Siemionow, V., Liu, J. Z., Sahgal, V., & Yue, G. (2004). From mental power to muscle power-gaining strength by using the mind. *Neuropsychologia , 42* (7), 944-956.

Richter, M., Eck, J., Straube, T., Miltner, W., & Weiss, T. (2010). Do words hurt? Brain activation during the processing of pain-related words. *PAIN* (148), 198-205.

Rosenhan, D. (1973, Jan). On Being Sane In Insane Places. *Science ,* 250-258.

Schapira, K., McClelland, H. A., Griffiths, N. R., & Newell, D. J. (1970). Study on the Effects of Tablet Colour in the Treatment of Anxiety States. *British Medical Journal* .

Seligman, M. (1998). *Learned Optimism.* Pocket Books.

Sidaway B., (. T. (2005). Can Mental Practice Increase Ankle Dorsiflexor Torque? *Physical Therapy* , *85* (10), 1053-1060.

Singleton N., B. R. (2000). *Psychiatric Morbidity among Adults living in Private Households.* Office for National Statistics, London.

Woolley, C. S., Gould, E., Frankfurt, M., & McEwen, B. S. (1990). Naturally occurring fluctuation in dendritic spine density on adult hippocampal pyramidal neurons. *Journal of Neuroscience* , 4035-4039.

Yapko, M. (2009). *Depression Is Contagious.* Free Press.

Other Publications/Courses by Phil Parker

The Ten Questions To Ask For Success
Phil's first book covers the core aspects of how to get success by using the most powerful questions in the world. This book has already inspired some of the world's leaders, and has been read all around the globe.

An Introduction to the Lightning Process
This book has been designed both as an essential first step for those intending to take a Lightning Process seminar and also as a resource for discovering more about how this unique training programme can make a difference in anyone's life.

CD Audio Programmes
His CD titles are designed to help you with every aspect of your life, covering topics such as de-stressing, building confidence, stopping smoking, weight loss and pregnancy support and more. For a full list please visit: **http://store.philparker.org**

Courses
Phil is constantly working to create new courses with easy access to all for the latest life changing ideas. These include:
- The Dû seminar - Learning how to use the Dû
- The Lightning Process (LP)
- Phil Parker Peak Performance (P4) - for business professionals and leaders in all fields
- NLP for Business - short and longer certified courses
- Language as Medicine - a seminar for health care professionals to learn how to use words to assist the healing process

For the full and latest information please go to the website: **www.philparker.org**.